John Abbott

After a varied career as an actor in theatre, film and television, John Abbott became a teacher of acting. He is Head of Academic Studies at the ArtsEd School of Acting in London, where he teaches Shakespeare, Stand Up and Improvisation.

Other Titles in this Series

John Abbott

THE IMPROVISATION BOOK

How to Conduct Successful Improvisation Sessions

NICK HERN BOOKS
London
www.nickhernbooks.co.uk

A NICK HERN BOOK

The Improvisation Book
first published in Great Britain in 2007
by Nick Hern Books Limited
14 Larden Road, London W3 7ST

Copyright © 2007 John Abbott

John Abbott has asserted his moral right
to be identified as the author of this work

Cover designed by Peter Bennett
Typeset by Country Setting, Kingsdown, Kent, CT14 8ES
Printed and bound in Great Britain by J.H. Haynes and Co. Ltd

A CIP catalogue record for this book is available from
the British Library

ISBN 978 1 85459 961 2

Contents

For Jane

Author's Note

I WORKED AS AN ACTOR FOR MOST OF MY LIFE IN ALL AREAS of the profession. At one time I was a member of the Royal Shakespeare Company and at another time I was the vicar in *Emmerdale Farm*. I still get royalties and fan mail for my appearance in four episodes of *Doctor Who* in the seventies and I spent twenty minutes in front of the camera filming a scene for *Four Weddings and a Funeral*.

A high point in my acting career was touring *The Tempest* with Mark Rylance's company Phoebus Cart and a low point was having to quack like a duck to sell toilet cleaner on Dutch television. Between a mixed bag of professional jobs I have been involved in quite a lot of poorly paid artistic and/or experimental perform-ance projects, a few of which could possibly have altered people's theatrical expectations.

Then I gave up acting and started teaching. As ever, the elders of the tribe pass on their survival skills to the younger generation.

I would like to thank all the students I have ever taught for their energy and enthusiasm in my classes. I experimented with some bizarre prototype Improvisation Cards, and my students always tried to make them work – they were even positive about some of my less-successful home-made games and exercises. Thanks for that.

I would also like to thank Amanda Brennan because she was the one who said, 'Come and teach Improvisation at the Kensington and Chelsea College' when I had absolutely no experience.

And, of course, special thanks to Jane Harrison, without whom . . .

Then, if it wasn't for Nick Hern, this book would have been a confused mess. Thanks for such detailed work, Nick (and for the grammar lesson). Thanks also to everyone else at Nick's place for their different skills, particularly Matt Applewhite who has kept me focused and on track, and who has found ways to produce a 'book with cut-out cards in the back' which is more stylish than I could have possibly imagined.

JOHN ABBOTT

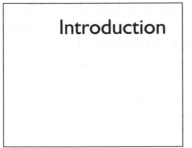

Introduction

I FIRST BECAME AWARE OF THE POTENTIAL OF IMPROVISATION when I saw Dustin Hoffman in the film *Midnight Cowboy*. There he is with his full-flight characterisation of Ratso, hobbling down a street in New York, smoking a cigarette and jabbering his streetwise scripted lines very truthfully and animatedly to Jon Voight. This scene is filmed with a long lens – the type that is like a telescope and makes it look as if the actors arc hardly moving towards you at all. In fact, the camera is so far away that the people on the street aren't even aware that any filming is taking place. Suddenly, just as the two actors are crossing a side street, a yellow cab lurches into view and jams on its brakes to avoid hitting them. Without breaking concentration, Dustin Hoffman turns round and hits the bonnet of the cab; his cigarette flies out of his mouth; he gestures wildly and shouts, 'Hey . . . I'm walkin' here . . . I'm walkin' here . . . Up yours, you sonofabitch.' The cab driver starts to shout back at him and Hoffman yells, 'You don't talk to me that way . . . Get out of here.' He then turns back to Jon Voight, grabs him by the arm to keep him walking and says, 'Don't worry about that . . . Actually, that ain't a bad way to pick up insurance, you know.' And they carry on down the street. It's a magic moment, because the audience senses that something real has just happened and that they have observed uncontrived, unrestrained 'life', and it is exciting and stimulating.

The only film Dustin Hoffman had made before *Midnight Cowboy* was *The Graduate* in which he played a character in his early twenties. Dustin Hoffman was over thirty at the time,

3

having spent ten years or so working in theatres in New York. Some of this theatre work had used explorative rehearsal techniques such as improvisation, so when he appeared to be nearly knocked down by that cab in *Midnight Cowboy*, rather than abandoning the shot, his improvisation skills clicked into place: he kept in character; he carried on talking; he made up his own script; and as a result the scene took on a new and unexpected life.

The ability to improvise allows the actor to stay 'in the moment' whatever might happen.

Of course, we have all become used to hearing improvised dialogue in films even if we aren't aware of it. The technique was explored during the sixties and seventies by the American actor/ director, John Cassavetes, in his low-budget, independently produced films like *Faces*, *Shadows* and *Husbands*, in which he often used improvisation to create dialogue. More recently, the British director Mike Leigh has constructed his films by using his actors' improvisation skills to create characters, invent dialogue and explore relationships from which he – and they – ultimately construct a plot. He has created some outstanding work using this method, including *Abigail's Party*, *Secrets and Lies* and *Vera Drake*.

So What is Improvisation?

Apart from its use in theatre and film, perhaps the word is most commonly associated with music. Indian classical music, for instance, is based on the 'raga', where the musicians improvise round a given set of notes; folk music is often improvised round a central theme, both melodically and lyrically; and, of course, jazz relies heavily on the musicians' ability to explore and improvise around both the melody and the chord structure of a tune. When musicians improvise they decide the notes they are going to play at more or less the same moment that they play them. They are not reading the music from a page, they are making it up as they go along. They are improvising. But whatever notes they decide to play, there is usually a strong musical framework for them to improvise within. A structure. A set of rules that must be obeyed. Sometimes these rules are bent; sometimes they are abandoned for a while; sometimes they are abused and scorned; but they are always there, lurking beneath the surface, holding everything in place. For without rules we tend towards anarchy.

And the joy of musical improvisation is twofold. In the first instance, the musician is allowing the Muse to take over. He or she finds that the music sometimes seems to write itself, the improvised tune appears out of the blue and can be more inspired and beautiful than a tune that is painstakingly crafted. And in the second instance the audience is observing a moment of artistic creation as it actually takes place. They are 'there at the time', and the joy of artistic creation is shared between the musician and the audience. It is a shared emotional experience. It can make you laugh or it can make you cry. It can be exciting; it can be moving; it can be shocking; but whatever emotion it inspires, it is alive. It is life itself.

And what is the actor trying to achieve in performance if it isn't 'life itself?'

There are several ways that improvisation can be used in the context of acting. We are familiar with the idea of actors improvising in front of an audience from television programmes like *Whose Line Is It Anyway?* This form of improvisation is often known as 'Theatre Games' or 'TheatreSports' and is usually performed by two or three comedians who are given a set of circumstances and/or characters from which to create a few minutes of improvised entertainment that can often turn into wild, anarchic comedy. The audience is continually aware that the actors are performing, and the joy lies in seeing how witty and imaginative their creations can be. Truth is often abandoned in favour of knockabout humour and funny lines. The actors who improvise in this way are often very skilful performers with strong imaginations and a powerful sense of danger, and the results can be wildly entertaining. However, 'TheatreSports' is not the kind of improvisation technique I will be discussing in this book.

This book is an examination of a more truthful form of improvisation which actors sometimes need in order to explore text, to build character, to create scenes and to perform in a realistic manner.

Actors are often afraid of improvisation because they feel they have to be entertaining or that they have to 'make something happen'. But although a certain amount of nerves and danger is always present in any rehearsal or performance, being afraid can be an enormous block to the imagination. So the most important thing in learning how to improvise is to get rid of that fear and allow the creative instinct to shine.

In order to do this, actors have to learn to trust their basic skills:

- They have to pretend to be someone else and then be truthful to the character they are pretending to be.

- They have to imagine they are in another situation and allow their characters to behave the way they would if the situation was really happening.

- They have to know what their characters want and then let that 'objective' affect the way their characters behave.

- And finally, they have to realise that their improvisations don't have to be interesting or entertaining: they just have to be truthful.

Having learned how to be truthful, actors can then learn ways of working together in an improvisation to build the plot and change the rhythms within an improvised scene. They can learn how to explore and create without losing the essence of realism.

When they have become comfortable with this approach, actors can also use improvisation to explore character, relationships and situations when they are working on texts. There are several techniques that can be used for this purpose. Directors will often 'hot-seat' a character. This is when the actor 'becomes' the character while the rest of the cast asks questions which are not addressed in the script itself in order to build up layers of characterisation. Sometimes a director will then improvise scenes from the play during the early explorative stage of rehearsal, so the actors get a greater understanding of the shape of a scene. On other occasions the director will make up situations that aren't actually in the play, so the actors can have a deeper understanding of the relationships between the characters. And sometimes, in order to explore the emotional changes that a character is going through in a scene, a director will set up an improvisation that deals with a particular emotion, but which has no direct connection with the plot of play. The actors will then be able to tap into the 'sense memory' of that emotion when they next rehearse the scene. When directors ask actors to improvise in this way, a commitment to reality and truth is the most valuable tool an actor can bring to the work.

As I mentioned earlier when I was talking about Mike Leigh, improvisation can also be used to write scripts. For instance, the actors can be required to create characters from observation and then build these characters through 'hot-seating'. The director will then set up a situation where two characters might meet, and the actors are asked to improvise a scene to see what happens. The scene can then be discussed, edited and re-improvised until it has some sort of shape. Sometimes a writer will be employed to make a script from these improvisations. One improvised scene can lead on to another and so on until a whole play has been constructed.

Improvisation is also often used during film-making. Sometimes in order to bring life to a scene, a film director will ask the actors to improvise around the script. If the actors are skilful in the technique, then the film can really take on the textures and rhythms of reality.

Finally, of course, this kind of truthful improvisation can be performed for an audience. And although the results can sometimes be humorous, the real joy of a reality-based performance improvisation is that it can also be moving, exciting, dramatic, absorbing, romantic and thought-provoking. In fact, an improvised performance can give an audience the whole range of emotional responses that they would experience if they were watching a text-based performance.

So what is there to learn? Improvisation seems so easy. Just make up the dialogue as you go along. A bit nerve-wracking if you're not used to it but what else is there to it?

Well, there's the main problem. Improvisation can be a *nerve-racking experience*. In fact, for some people, it can be quite frightening. There are a lot of actors whose blood runs cold when they are asked to improvise. They'll do it, of course they will, but they won't feel comfortable. They'll feel the spotlight has become an interrogation lamp and is blinding their creativity: like rabbits in the headlights of a car, they just freeze. It's not that they can't do it; they can to a degree, but their inspiration is blocked and inhibited by anxiety or fear.

The aim of this book is to take away that fear. That's all. And in order to take away that fear there are a number of exercises and techniques that are easy to learn, easy to apply and easy to put into practice. And the more technique that actors have, the less fear; and the less fear they have, the more they will be free to be creative and original.

I teach on the B.A. (Hons) in Acting at the Arts Educational School in London, where the improvisation training is closely linked to actor training, so, although this is a book about improvisation, a lot of the things that are discussed as improvisation techniques apply to text-based acting as well. Trusting, listening, emotions, having objectives, etc. etc. However, to avoid confusion I have used the term 'improviser' throughout this book rather than 'actor' or 'student', although a lot of the time these words are interchangeable.

And that leads to the next question. Is this book for actors, or is it for directors, or is it for teachers? Well, in a way it's for all of them. And it's also for people who just want to play games. Each chapter deals with an area of technique that can be explored, practised and refined in order to give an actor the tools to improvise truthfully, creatively and without fear. As such, it is written primarily to be used by a *teacher* to create a series of classes. On the other hand, a small group of *actors* could get together to practise the techniques on their own. Or a *director* could use some of the exercises to help the cast discover more about the characters in whatever play they are rehearsing, be it Shakespeare, Pinter or a new devised piece.

Each chapter is, in fact, based on one of the technique classes that I teach at the ArtsEd and is divided into three distinct sections. In order to underpin the practical exploration of technique with a mildly philosophical or anecdotal illustration of the thinking behind it, I begin each chapter with a personal journey into my own memories and experiences to find some sort of correlation between parts of my life and the particular technique I want to discuss. Then in the second section of each chapter I talk about how this rather cerebral approach can have a practical application for an improviser. The third section of each chapter contains a set of carefully explained 'exercises' that can either be used individually to explore the technique under discussion or collectively as a recipe for a class. Finally, each chapter ends with 'improvisations' which allow the improvisers to put the learned techniques into practice.

For the purposes of this book, an 'exercise' is something the teacher has control over and can adjust while it is taking place. And may or may not include improvisation. But an 'improvisation', once it has started, belongs to the improvisers and shouldn't be interfered with at all, until it has finished. Then, of course, it can be the subject of discussion and analysis.

After each exercise or improvisation, I have included what I call 'Debriefing' notes. These are supposed to be points of discussion that a teacher can have with a group of students about the purpose of the exercises. I don't usually explain why we are doing various exercises until after we have done them. Most of the people who attend these classes have come to the school because they want to be actors rather than improvisers, and they can be quite nervous of improvisation. In the past they have often been expected to be funny or to be entertaining and to have had their improvisations closely scrutinised and criticised, so naturally they have become inhibited. I try to let the work sneak up on them through games and simple exercises, so they find themselves doing something quite serious and concentrated without knowing how they got to that point. Saying, 'Today you will be doing a group improvisation about people being ship-wrecked on a raft, to see how well you relate to each other,' at the beginning of the class would throw everyone into a panic. So I start with some silly games and subtly move on to some simple solo acting exercises, which in turn lead to more dramatic solo acting exercises and before they know it they are in the middle of a dramatic group improvisation without any pressure. (This series of games and exercises is explained in detail in Chapter 2: Trusting Others.) If they had been aware of the 'goal' before they started, some of them would have become tense and inhibited.

But, of course, it's important for them to understand why they are doing these classes, so a discussion afterwards makes them realise what they have achieved and how useful and productive each individual technique can be.

You will notice that I take strong control of the early classes, often 'talking them through' an exercise or improvisation while they are doing it. They are expected to use their acting skills to imagine they are in a particular situation and to behave accord-ingly, yet at the same time they mustn't lose concentration while I describe various changes or sensory experiences which I want them to think about and incorporate. As part of the description of the exercises, I have included examples of the things I might say and the way I might say them in order to clarify this particu-lar way of working.

I would also recommend that teachers join in some of the games in the early stages, since this takes pressure off nervous people.

As the course progresses and the improvisers develop a greater con-fidence and creativity, it is possible for the teacher to take a back seat, interfere less and less, observe their work and subsequently lead analy-tical discussions.

At the end of the book there is an Appendix with a selection of warm-up games and exercises that can be used at the start of a session to 'shake out the cobwebs' and put people in a creative frame of mind. Most of these games have no specific purpose other than to bring the group together and focus their concentration. They can be used as and when necessary since they are not connected to any particular technique or topic of exploration.

You will also notice that I sometimes suggest dividing the group into two smaller groups. I usually work with about eighteen students, so that would mean they would be nine or ten people in each group. If I suggest three smaller groups, there would be about five or six people in each group.

The Improvisation Cards

Anyone who has taught improvisation on a regular basis will have found that the continual need for new improvisation scenarios has been a great drain on their imagination. You can buy books of improvisation scenarios, but they are often rather specific and not necessarily of much use in more general classes. So in order to make my life easier, I created some Improvisation Cards. These cards are 'Mix 'n' Match', and can be used to make an enormous variety of improvisations simply by rearranging the ingredients. (The cards are all reproduced at the back of this book.)

THE SCENARIO CARDS

There are sixty-three Scenario Cards, split into three sets: *Simple*, *Complex* and *Extreme*. With these scenarios it is better not to let people try to run before they can walk. Start with the Simple Scenarios and only when they have been fully explored, move on to the Complex Scenarios. Similarly, save the Extreme Scenarios until you are absolutely sure that you have finished with the Complex Scenarios. (As you read the book, you will find that I have indicated when it is appropriate to start using each set of Scenario Cards.) Most of the scenarios on these cards are for two people; however, there are some that can be used for three or even more (i.e. 'Strangers in an all-night café at 5.00 in the morning.') When two or more people are preparing to do an improvisation, the information on the Scenario Cards is usually shared with the whole group.

S The SIMPLE SCENARIOS can be used for a lot of the exercises in this book and are basically situations that the improviser should be reasonably familiar with. Shopping. Friends. School. Work. Etc.

C The COMPLEX SCENARIOS are situations that are still in the realm of a familiar reality but that haven't necessarily been within the experience of the improvisers. Consequently they require the improvisers to use their imagination rather than their experience (i.e. 'Musicians in a band.' 'Strangers stuck in a lift.' 'A kidnapper and a victim.' Etc.). As I said, the Complex Scenarios should only be used when the improvisers can confidently tap into the truth of unfamiliar situations.

IE The third set of Scenario Cards are the EXTREME SCENARIOS and should only be used after all the techniques have been absorbed and all the other scenarios have been fully explored. In fact they are probably best left until after Chapter 16: Interruptions, because these Extreme Scenarios often work better with a larger number of people. Two or three main characters can start the improvisation with the rest of the group becoming part of the 'scene' by 'interrupting' or joining in.

The scenarios in this third set are what could best be described as fantasy, but in fact they have to be played with an incredible dedication to truth and reality, otherwise they just become an excuse to have a laugh. I always refer to the film *Alien* where the newborn baby alien bursts out of John Hurt's stomach during a meal and runs off across the floor. Although this is not in the realm of any of our 'realities', the scene was acted with a total commitment to truth and as a result was shocking, dangerous and totally believable.

These Extreme Scenarios can be risky if used too early; no one will learn anything. However, they are familiar cinematic situations –

Aliens. Invisible Men. Superheroes. Goblins. Cave-dwellers, etc. – and as I said, the improvisers have to be quite experienced in order to play them truthfully.

THE CHARACTER CARDS

These cards should be used with the Scenario Cards to give the improvisers a sense of character. I have tried to be both subtle and generic in creating these cards. They should indicate a 'sort' of person. However, to use them correctly they must be treated with caution. I will explain how to use them in more detail in Chapter 9: Character, but suffice it to say now that a melancholic person is *sometimes* happy and that a hypochondriac doesn't *always* talk about their health. These cards are *indications of character* rather than one-dimensional characterisations that must be played exclusively and relentlessly.

USING THE CARDS

First of all, two improvisers will select a Scenario Card and tell everyone what the scenario is. Then each improviser will select, and read, a Character Card. They usually keep the information on this card to themselves, since it is more interesting for the other improviser in a scene to see their partner's character unfold. However, this is not a rule and in some circumstances it is important for each person to know the character traits of the other person. If they are siblings, for instance, they would obviously know quite a lot about each other.

The great thing about this 'Mix 'n' Match' system is that they generate an enormous number of variations. If, for instance, an improviser has already used the 'Kidnapper and Victim' Scenario Card in a previous improvisation, he or she will not only be with a new partner, but they will now pick an entirely new character. Their partner will also have a different character and consequently the second improvisation will turn out to be quite unlike any previous 'Kidnapper and Victim' improvisation that has gone before.

EDITING THE CHARACTER CARDS

Some of the Character Cards are quite subtle and open to interpretation and they should be used with discretion (see Chapter 9: Character). Depending on the maturity of the group, I would suggest that some, or all, of the following cards could be removed from the pack in case they are misunderstood: Searcher; Holidaymaker; Person at a crossroads; Fallen star; Physical person; Lover; Winner; Elusive person.

Notes for the Improvisation Sessions

ARGUMENTS

I am pretty opposed to improvised arguments. These arguments feel fabulous to the improvisers. They think they are doing 'real acting' because they get to shout and scream and hurl abuse at each other. They are very popular with teenagers. I call them 'You bitch – You bastard' impros, because that just about sums up their content. The trouble with improvised arguments is that they have nowhere to go because no one backs down and the argument just churns on and on. However, disagreements *can* sometimes occur during an improvisation. When that happens I ask the students to look for another way to 'win' their argument or to put their point across rather than just by shouting. Having said that, there are two occasions when I ask them to improvise an argument, but on each occasion it's only for a short time and the argument is an important step to another exercise. The first time I ask them to improvise an argument is described in Chapter 5: Adjusting the Scenario, where I use it to prepare them for a variety of disagreements. I want to get the basic shouting-match out of their system before they start and I take the opportunity to explain how limiting this sort of improvisation can be. The second time an argument can break out is in Chapter 13: Releasing the Imagination, where three people are trying to 'top' each other's inventive ideas. However, this is more of a shouting session than a basic argument, and can actually become very creative.

BLOCKING

The other thing to avoid is what Keith Johnstone refers to as 'blocking'. It's very simple really. If one improviser says, 'It's raining', and the other says, 'No it isn't. The sun is shining,' they are left with nowhere to go except endless repetition. One of them must be mad or deliberately trying to pick a fight. And we don't want that! But although this sounds like a simple problem to solve, and could easily be overcome by saying 'Yes' to any suggestion, it's not quite as straightforward as that. When two people are improvising, they will both have their creative juices flowing and making-up stories and relationships in their heads before they have a chance to talk about them. So at the beginning of an improvisation, one person may have decided that the other is their long-lost sister; they want to know what has happened to her over the last ten years and could start the improvisation with a line like: 'What happened to you? What have you been doing?' The second person may have an entirely different scenario going through their heads and say, 'Oh, hi Mum. Sorry I just went to the shops to buy some milk.' At that point the first improviser has to make a massive adjustment to their mental scenario otherwise we get a 'blocked' improvisation. The first person can't just say, 'But I haven't seen you for ten years and anyway you are my sister', she just has to accept the new scenario and build from there. Once something has been said, then it has to be true.

REMOVING THE PRESSURE

A lot of the time, especially during the early sessions, I have pairs of people improvising in different parts of the room at the same time. This is to take the pressure off them and allow them to get used to improvising truthfully without being observed. In the past, people have often been under such pressure to 'deliver' during an improvisation class that it's now important for them to understand that for these improvisation sessions it doesn't matter whether anyone is watching or not. It's just up to the improvisers to find the truth of the scene.

PAIRING UP

In the early sessions I allow the group to divide themselves into pairs so that they can work with the people they particularly like. However, I continually ask them to find new partners for each new exercise so that they can learn from working with a variety of people. As the sessions progress I start making the pairings myself, so they are working with as many different people as possible. I do this by getting them to stand in a line in a particular order (the first letter of their second name, or the first letter of the name of their favourite actor, or their mother or whatever). And then I go down the line pairing up people who are standing next to each other.

DIVIDING THE GROUP

If I want to divide the group into two smaller groups, I often ask them to get into pairs and then ask one of them to be A and the other one to be B. Then I get all the As to go to one end of the room and all the Bs to go to the other. This helps to mix them up so that best friends aren't always in the same group. A similar thing can be done to divide the group into *three* smaller groups, by initially asking them to get into groups of three and calling themselves A, B or C.

GENDER ISSUES

Some of the scenarios would indicate that the two improvisers should be of different genders (i.e. 'A blind date.' 'A long-term couple, breaking up, divide their belongings.' Etc.). When I use these cards I always say that gender is not an issue. By that I mean that two people of the same gender can be on a blind date or be a long-term couple breaking up. However, I strongly discourage sexual stereotypes. An improviser can look at someone of the same gender and imagine they love them in exactly the same way that they can look at someone of the opposite gender and imagine the same thing. Both ways they are 'acted' emotions and feelings, and all the improviser has to do is search for the truth of the emotions in the same way that they search for the truth of how they might feel if they were a plumber or a doctor or a hairdresser.

However, depending on the maturity of the group, gender *could* be an issue. If that is the case, I would suggest that the Scenario Cards are sorted out in an appropriate fashion before a session begins, so that gender issues don't inhibit creativity.

NOT BEING CLEVER

Finally, what improvisers must understand is that they are not expected to be 'clever' in an improvisation. In fact, they should force themselves to stop trying to be clever. There is no point in trying to impress anyone because the only purpose of this sort of improvisation is for them to learn something about their character, their character's life or their character's relationships with other people.

All they have to do is imagine that they are a particular person in a particular situation; listen to what is being said to them and react truthfully. It's as simple as that.

I

Trusting Yourself

If you have ever watched a potter shaping a pot at the wheel, or a baby examining a flower for the first time, you will begin to understand how absolutely absorbing another person's concentration can be. We all love to see other people being totally engaged by whatever they are doing: the athlete focusing for the 100-metre dash; the *Mastermind* contestant concentrating on a difficult question; the snooker player engrossed in the geometry of his next shot. As observers we too become focused, concentrated and absorbed.

A few years ago there was an exhibition of Tibetan art in London. As part of the exhibition a group of Tibetan monks created a sand mandala. The word 'mandala' is Sanskrit for circle, and a sand mandala is an intricate circular symmetrical picture drawn in coloured sand. It is often a symbolic illustration of a palace with four gates, facing the four corners of the Earth and is representative of 'man' or 'woman' in the world. These mandalas are used as a support for meditation.

To make the mandala, the monks first sketched out the pattern of the picture on a flat table about eight foot square. When that was finished, three or four of the monks worked at colouring in the patterns and shapes of the mandala using nothing but brightly coloured, dyed sand. They used a series of traditional copper funnels called chakpurs to pour out the sand. These funnels have a very fine hole at the end and a ridged edge, so that by moving a wooden stick up and down the bumps of the ridged edge the coloured sand falls out grain by grain. The monks have to be very careful as they colour in the mandala because they cannot make a mistake. There is no rubbing out or painting over. A sand mandala takes several days to create, and the monks meditate as they work – or to be more accurate: their work itself is their meditation – and as a result their concentration is very intense. While the monks worked, visitors to the exhibition were allowed to watch them, and the 'audience' were as intrigued by the commitment, self-belief and pure concentration of the monks as they were by the developing work of art.

The mandala was finished after about a week, and the monks lifted it up and carried it carefully to the Thames where they ceremonially poured the sand into the water as a blessing for the health and healing of the people of London.

They did it for us, and they did it for themselves.

We live in a society of critics. Newspapers, magazines and television programmes continually need things to write about, and every journalist has to have an opinion to express. Is the latest recording by this or that band as good as their last? Is such and such a politician making the right decisions or the wrong decisions (and by the way, is his murky private life acceptable or not?). And now there seem to be hundreds of programmes on television which have a panel of experts giving their opinion on the talent of an amateur singer who wants to be a star. And what is more, everyone at home can phone in and give their judgement too (via a premium-rate telephone call, of course). Everyone is a critic nowadays. No wonder performers get nervous.

The Tibetan monks didn't get nervous.

Why not? What's the difference?

The difference is that the monks believe in what they are doing. They believe in themselves. They concentrate on the job in hand. They put all other thoughts out of their mind.

HOW CAN ACTORS LEARN TO BELIEVE IN THEMSELVES AND concentrate during an improvisation when expectations are so great? When people watch an improvisation they always seem as if they are going to have an opinion. They seem as if they are ready to criticise. Did the improvisers create good characters?

Were they able to keep talking? Did they have good imaginations? Were they funny? Who was the best?

Who was the best? Ouch!

Positive Feelings

For any kind of performer these problems cannot be solved overnight. Many creative people continually question the worth of their creations. But if you are leading a group of people through an exploration of improvisation techniques, the first thing you need to do is to help them develop a positive mental attitude to improvisation. The best way to do this is to encourage them to tap into the times when they felt good about themselves. When people are with a new group they often feel quite nervous and unsure of themselves until everyone else knows who they are and why they are there. So help them get to know each other. If they are complete strangers, make sure they get to know each other's names, and at the same time, make sure you learn their names as quickly as you can. Use their names whenever possible. Encourage everyone to find out a little about everyone else. If they are interested in other people, other people will be interested in them. Get them to ask each other questions and encourage them to be forthcoming in their answers. Make it fun. Take the pressure off.

The next step is to help people to work on a positive mental attitude about themselves. They are probably used to acting, even in a small way, so they will be able to 'act' positive feelings if you talk them through the details: a positive stride; positive thoughts; optimistic feelings; etc. And the more they practise 'acting' feeling positive, the more positive they will become.

Positive feelings are important and need to be reaffirmed on a regular basis.

What is Improvisation?

First of all, people need to know what improvisation really means before they can start doing it. Encourage them to think about what it is. Encourage them to think about what it is *for*. Let them make their own decisions. Let them express their own opinions. Do they like watching improvisation? Do they like doing it? Encourage discussion. Encourage them to speak and encourage them to listen.

If people are allowed to express their own ideas, they start to feel positive about themselves.

Having allowed the group to discuss improvisation and the various forms that it can take, it is important to clarify the kind of improvisation they will be exploring in these sessions. Keep positive about their ideas and experiences, but make sure they understand that this is improvisation for exploration of *character* and *relationships*; it is not improvisation for entertainment. Make it particularly clear to them that *they don't have to be funny.*

The Ground Rules

Finally, identify the ground rules of these improvisation sessions. How long is each improvisation? When does it stop? Do they need props? Could they be animals? Make sure they understand the guidelines – the foundations of an improvisation. If the foundations are solid then they can build confidently on top of them without the fear of collapse.

The rules that I use are simple.

1. IMPROVISATIONS ARE USUALLY FOUR MINUTES LONG. I time them with a stopwatch and finish them, even in mid-sentence, when the time is up. In the early stages of the training, four minutes is long enough to explore a particular improvisation technique, and yet it is short enough for everyone in a group to have a chance to try out the technique for themselves.

2. IMPROVISATIONS ONLY END WHEN I SAY SO. Sometimes people think they have nothing more to say and they will just stop improvising. But why stop? Life doesn't stop, and an improvisation should be like life. Inexperienced improvisers usually stop when things start to get difficult

or they can't think what to say next, but in fact that is just the time when interesting things start to happen because the improvisers have to start being creative and exploring uncharted territory.

3. DON'T TALK TO PEOPLE WHO AREN'T THERE. If there is a difficult moment in an improvisation and people don't know what to do next, they will often turn to an imaginary waiter and ask for the menu, or start having a one-sided conversation with a passing policeman or whatever. But what's the point of that? That's just working on your own. Why do that when there are real people – other improvisers – who will give you a response and work with you? This leads to the next rule.

4. DON'T TALK ON IMAGINARY TELEPHONES. I know telephones have become a major part of everyone's life, and not allowing improvisers to talk on the telephone can sometimes be untrue to life. But as above, people start having one-way conversations and are actually just talking to themselves. What good is that unless you are working on a one-person show? (Actually, even if someone is exploring character for a one-person show, it would be far more revealing to get another actor to improvise scenes with them than to have them talk on a telephone.)

5. DON'T TRY TO EXPLAIN OR CLARIFY ANYTHING TO WHOEVER MIGHT BE WATCHING; JUST BE TRUTHFUL. Classic examples of 'explaining' things are when people yawn to show they are tired; look at their watch to indicate they are waiting for someone; roll their eyes and sigh to show that they are exasperated; drum their fingers to show they are impatient; or scratch their head to show they are thinking. The other thing people do is to try to talk their thoughts when they are on their own in an improvisation. 'I think I'd like a cup of tea.' 'I wonder where Dave is, he's supposed to be here.' 'I'm so happy.' Or they try to fill in the details of mimed props. 'Here, hold this parcel that the postman just delivered.' 'I'm

wearing a light suit because it's hot.' None of these explanations are necessary and most of the time they are unrealistic. Improvisers just have to believe in their own creations and anyone who is watching will believe in them too.

6. MIME PROPS. Then you can do anything and be anywhere you like.

7. DON'T BE ANIMALS.

8. DON'T GET INTO IMPROVISED, ABUSIVE ARGUMENTS. (See 'Arguments' in the Introduction.)

9. DON'T 'BLOCK'. If the other improviser says something, then you have to accept it as the truth. (See 'Blocking' in the Introduction.)

10. ALWAYS USE YOUR OWN NAMES. It's so much easier than trying to remember made-up names.

(Later on in the training when a group is working well together, I do allow the improvisers to talk to imaginary people; in fact, I encourage it. But on those occasions, one of the people watching the improvisation will get up, join in briefly and be the waiter or the policeman or whatever. Or one of the observers will become a voice on the other end of a telephone. But a lot needs to be learned before that can work properly. This is explained in more detail in Chapter 16: Interruptions.)

So . . . Make sure they know the rules. Even John Coltrane obeyed the rules of whatever oriental scale he was exploring when he played his (apparently) wild saxophone improvisations.

If improvisers know what they are supposed to be doing and they feel at their best, then all they have to do is do it. *There is no right or wrong. Nothing is better or worse than anything else. All that exists is their own creative input. And that is all there is.*

They just have to trust themselves.

Exercises

The following exercises may seem incredibly naive, but for people who haven't worked together before, they can be extremely reassuring because they are so simple to do. Remember, naivety is a valuable resource for an actor or an improviser to tap into. It releases inhibitions and is a reminder of childhood – a time when you were the centre of the universe and felt totally confident in yourself.

I'm Jane with the Red Shoes

Get the group to stand in a circle, and ask each person to think of something very simple they could say about themselves. Then ask each of them to introduce themselves to the rest of the group one at a time, saying something like 'Hi, I'm Jane and I've got red shoes.' Everyone then has to shout back 'Hi Jane, who's got red shoes,' and then the next person round the circle has a go. It is important to keep this ridiculous exercise lively and positive. I usually start this off myself to show them how to do it, and then I join in enthusiastically with the response to each of the other introductions.

RATIONALE   *This is simply to get people to relax and have fun, but at the same time they are starting to learn each other's names.*

Introduce a Partner

Still standing in the circle, ask people to get into pairs where they stand. Then ask everybody at the same time to have a short conversation with their partner to make sure they know each other's names, and to learn some simple facts about each other. When they have done that, each person has to introduce their partner to the rest of the group and tell them what they have learned, e.g. 'This is Peter and he has three sisters. He comes from Oldham and his pet dog is called Bert.'

RATIONALE   *This game helps everyone learn a little more about each other. The names are used again, and a little more information is being shared. By getting someone else to do the introduction, it makes sure that people are listening to each other. They can't introduce their partner if they haven't been listening to what their partner said. It's also easier for some people to talk publicly about someone else, rather than talking about themselves.*

The Name Game

With the group standing in a circle, ask one person to walk towards another person anywhere across the circle, saying that person's name as they go, and taking their place in the circle when they get there. Then this second person has to walk towards a third person saying that person's name and taking their place, etc. etc. If it's a new group, tell them if they can't remember someone's name as they walk towards them, they can stage-whisper, 'What's your name?', and then shout it out joyfully when they are told what it is.

RATIONALE   *This is to get people to use each other's names. Sometimes I get two, three or even four people crossing the circle at the same time and shouting out names. Names are flying round the room and settling into the subconscious. (I usually take this opportunity to test the progress of my own knowledge of names by mentally repeating names and forcing myself to connect names with faces.)*

Brainstorming

Divide the group into four or five smaller groups and ask them to discuss the following:

1. What is improvisation?

2. What is improvisation for?

3. What experiences do they have of improvising?

4. What experiences do they have of watching improvisation?

After allowing all the smaller groups to discuss these points for ten to twenty minutes, ask everyone to sit in a circle so each small group can feed back the results of their discussions. This can lead to an open discussion with the whole group.

RATIONALE   By allowing people to talk, unobserved, in small groups it helps them to say what they really feel. In my experience, a lot of people are frightened of improvisation. They have often been expected to be entertaining or funny or inventive. During this discussion I take the opportunity to explain that no one has to be any of these things. As I said earlier, these sessions are not for entertainment. All the improvisers have to do is to try to be realistic. I also explain quite clearly what I am teaching improvisation for. I am teaching it as a tool for the actor. It is ultimately for the exploration of character, relationships and text.

I Feel Great!

With everyone working at the same time but each person working on their own, ask everyone to walk around the room and think about themselves.

Firstly, ask them to focus their concentration on their MIND and feel intelligent, witty and bright.

Secondly, ask them to focus their concentration on their BODY and feel healthy and strong.

And then ask them to focus their concentration on their DIRECTION and feel positive and purposeful.

Finally, ask them to put all three together and shout joyfully to the heavens: 'I feel great!'

I usually talk them through this exercise in something like the following manner:

'Walk around the room and think about the times when you felt mentally wide-awake. Think about the feelings you had when you felt witty and intelligent. Really concentrate. Look at the world and consciously observe and think about everything that you see. Who made this? How long has that been there? What is the history of the building you can see out of the window? Force yourself to be alert. Check out the details. Smile as your brain starts to work at its best. Have opinions about things without inhibitions. Do you REALLY like the clothing or haircuts that are fashionable at the moment? Do you REALLY like that crap programme on TV that you can't stop watching? Laugh at the wickedness of your individuality and your boldness of opinion. Your mind is sharp, witty and alive.

'Now start concentrating on your physical self. Breathe in the air and feel it giving you life. Feel it making you healthy and strong. Remember the times when you performed some physical feat without tiring. Maybe it was a brisk five-mile walk through the countryside on a fine spring morning; maybe it was clubbing till four in the morning. Pound your chest like Tarzan and bellow for joy at your strength and vitality. Jump up and punch the air in jubilant celebration and feel all your muscles spring into life so they can do whatever you physically require. Let the adrenaline flow through your body. You could do anything. You are healthy and strong.

'Now concentrate on the way you walk. Feel that your feet could take you wherever you want to go. They give you direction. They give you purpose. If you want to get anywhere, all you have to do is walk and your legs will take you there. See that interesting mark on the wall? See that chair by the door? All you have to do is walk towards them and the details and complexity of each and every object will become clearer and clearer. Your legs can take you anywhere you want to go and as you proceed they will increase your knowledge. Lengthen your stride. Swing your arms and just go. If you want to get somewhere all you have to do is walk there. If you want to get to the top, all you have to do is head in the right direction and take that journey one optimistic step after another. Feel purpose in your stride.

'Keep walking and start putting these feelings together. Focus on your mind and feel how intelligent and mentally sharp you are; focus on your body and feel your health and strength; focus on your physical movement through space and feel your sense of purpose. Mind. Body. Direction. Swap from one to the other and back again until you have all three working at the same time. See how you look. Check it out in the mirror. Check out how other people look in the room. See how fabulous they appear. There is a smile on your face and you feel just great. This is you at your best in all ways. Remember this feeling. You can have it whenever you want. It's how you felt when you set out in this world. It is how you need to feel to be at your most creative. Trust yourself. You are mentally alert; you are healthy and strong and you have a sense of purpose. The ups and downs of life have made you doubt these things, but it is only the negativity of other people who have made you doubt yourself.

'Now, with positive enthusiasm shout out "I feel great!" Shout it to the heavens. Shout it to the world. Keep saying it. "I feel great!" "I feel great!" Keep the positive feelings and keep saying this phrase.'

RATIONALE *By using a positive tone of voice to 'talk them through' these positive images and positive actions, the people in the group can use their imagination and their acting skills to explore positive emotions about themselves. I tell them that this exercise is a trick I use for myself if I have to go to an interview or an important meeting, in order to get myself in the right frame of mind.*

Improvisations

Three Steps to Improvisation

Step 1

Divide the group into pairs and ask each pair to have a chat about something simple: television programmes, food, clothes, etc. Have all the pairs doing this at the same time so no one feels they are being observed.

DEBRIEFING *Tell them that this is the* BASIS *of any improvisation. That's all there is to it:*

* *Having a conversation when you are asked to, instead of when you feel like it*

Step 2

Divide the group into new sets of pairs and ask everyone to think of a friend and the subject that friend likes to talk about: football, music, chocolate, etc. Then ask the pairs to have a chat, but each person must try to bring the conversation round to their friend's favourite subject. And talk about it the way their friend would. They shouldn't try to impersonate their friend, they should be themselves but they should say the things their friend likes to say. Again, have everyone doing this at the same time so no one feels they are being observed.

DEBRIEFING   *Tell them that this is the* ESSENCE *of any improvisation:*

- *Trying to get inside the head of another person*

- *Trying to think the way another person thinks*

Step 3

Divide the group into new sets of pairs and ask each pair to decide where they could be: on a busy station, in the countryside, in the pub, etc. And do the second step again using the favourite subject of a friend but this time in an imagined location. Again, all the pairs do this at the same time. No observation.

DEBRIEFING   *Tell them that is the* CREATIVITY *of improvisation:*

- *Chatting to another person*

- *Trying to think like someone else*

- *Pretending you are in a different location*

- *Pretending that the person you are talking to is someone else*

RATIONALE   *This is purely to introduce them to the simplicity of truthful improvisations. It is to help them overcome any fearful anticipation of performance improvisation that they might have brought with them to the session.*

Session Debriefing

That's all there is to improvisation: the rest is just refinements and techniques. For this sort of improvisation, the improvisers don't have to entertain. They don't have to be massively inventive or original. All they have to do is be truthful, react naturally and trust themselves.

2

Trusting Others

When I was a child I loved watching the Lone Ranger and his partner Tonto on television. There were a lot of cowboy shows on television in those days, and each cowboy hero had a sidekick who would help him out. The Cisco Kid had Pancho; Wyatt Earp had Doc Holliday; and Hopalong Cassidy had eleven different sidekicks during his career, the most memorable being played by Gabby Hayes. And it went beyond cowboy shows. Batman had Robin; Inspector Clouseau had Kato; Butch Cassidy had the Sundance Kid; and Frodo had three sidekicks – Merry, Pippin and Samwise. The list is endless. Robinson Crusoe had Man Friday; King Arthur had Lancelot; Doctor Who has had a succession of female assistants. Once you start thinking about it you realise that in order to get anything done in this world you need a trusty friend to help you out. Or trusty friends! How about The Three Musketeers, The Fab Four, The Famous Five, The Magnificent Seven, The Band of Brothers, The Knights of the Round Table, Robin Hood and his Merrie Men?

The thing about trusty friends, though, is that they have talents of their own. The mark of a true hero is to recognise the talents of his sidekicks and employ them to overcome the villains. They work together, they allow each other to use their individual skills, and they trust each other implicitly. Two (or more) heads are better than one.

ONE OF THE DANGERS FOR SOME INEXPERIENCED IMPROVISERS is that they feel they have to do it all on their own. They are doing their best to commit to some sort of reality, they are trying to be creative, but they feel that the success or failure of an improvisation is in their hands alone. Well, it isn't. They'll always have a trusty sidekick who also has talents and who is there to work with them; to support them; to be supported by them; to fill in the gaps and to help them overcome all difficulties.

It's vital that improvisers learn to trust each other and understand that their partners will be doing half the work.

Simple Trust Exercises

In order to explore and develop that trust, try starting with some basic trust exercises. Try simple physical contact exercises. Have people gently patting each other's backs. Massaging each other's shoulders. (Some people don't like being touched by comparative strangers, and if physical contact makes them tense it entirely defeats the object. For these people, patting their shoulders and back is best since that sort of contact is brief and fairly impersonal.)

Another thing you can do is to have one person shut their eyes and another lead them very carefully around the room. Ask the person with their eyes shut to talk about something. Maybe their favourite subject. Football. A soap opera. Whatever. As they talk they may forget that they have their eyes shut and as their minds wander through their favourite subjects they will start to associate pleasant thoughts with trust. There are a number of useful exercises in the Appendix of this book. Try games that involve people speaking to each other and sharing words, like '1, 2, 3' or 'Two People Talking at the Same Time'. You could also ask the whole group to work together and use 'Zip, Zap, Boing' or 'Down, Down, Baby'. (See Appendix: Warm-up Games and Exercises.)

Only when the individuals in the group start to feel confident with each other can they begin to explore improvisation creatively.

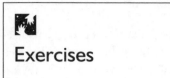

Exercises

Chair is Any Object

Ask the group to stand in a circle and place a chair in the middle of the circle. One at a time, each person has to step into the circle and use the chair as if it were an entirely different object. The rest of the people in the circle have to guess what the chair is supposed to be. It could be a cricket bat; it could be an earring; it could be a tractor; or it could be a hat. It could be anything their imagination wants it to be.

RATIONALE   *This exercise is to get the group using their imaginations, and having the courage to be observed. I usually start this off by miming that the chair is an earring, because that is so incongruous and it helps them get the idea that anything is possible. After that, anyone can step forward at any time and each person can have several turns. If some people appear to be holding back because they are nervous I usually end the exercise by asking people to use the chair one at a time round the circle. Or sometimes I ask them to do the exercise in pairs.*

Talk a Person Off the Chair

Ask the group to stand in a circle and ask one person to sit on a chair in the centre of the circle. One of the other people has to start an improvisation that will eventually get the other person to leave the chair. The person on the chair mustn't block the improvisation.

RATIONALE   *This exercise is interesting because it involves negotiation. If the person sitting on the chair abandons realistic reactions in order to 'win' the game and stay in the chair, then the two improvisers reach a stalemate. Like this:*

> *'There is a bomb under the chair!'*

> *'No there isn't.'*

'Yes there is, I can hear it ticking.'

'Well, I can't.'

'Well, have a look then, you can see it.'

'I can't bend down, I've got a bad back.'

'Oh my God, it's about to go off!'

'I don't care.'

'You don't care?'

'No, I'm going to stay in this chair as long as I like.'

'I'll give you a million pounds if you get out of the chair.'

'I don't want it.'

Oh yeah? They wouldn't get out of a chair for a million pounds?

On the other hand, the person who wants the chair mustn't give up too easily because the improvisation will go nowhere. As in:

'Can you give me your seat? I'm pregnant.'

'No. I'm really tired; I've just run the London Marathon.'

'Oh sorry. You must be exhausted. I'll ask someone else.'

This is a dead-end improvisation that has actually been finished before it has started. But even in those few lines there is a lot of material that the improvisers could use to move the improvisation forward. Pregnancy. Tiredness. The London Marathon. These subjects could take the improvisation in a number of different directions.

Allow the improvisers to try this game several times until they start to get the balance right.

Walking on Different Surfaces

Ask everyone to walk around the room, weaving in and out of each other. Tell them that each person should be working on their own, and trying to imagine that they are in the different environments you are about to describe. They should be guided through each environment by, first of all, a description of the ground they are walking on, and then an analysis of the sensory experiences of each particular environment. Ask them to react to each experience with their own imagination and physicality. I usually talk them through the four seasons as follows:

Autumn

'Imagine you are walking in the country along the side of a rolling hill covered in grass. Feel the sensation through your feet of walking across a field. Is the grass springy? Is it wet? Are there tufts and bumps? Keep walking, keep exploring. It is autumn. Use your imagination to explore all the sensory sensations of walking in the country at this time of year. What does the air smell like? How cold is it? Is there any wind? What can you hear? What can you see? Imagine the sun is shining but the air has a slight chill. Now imagine that you have come to a wood or forest and you decide to walk into it. Experience the difference sensations. The trees shade the sun so it is darker and colder. The smells are different. Moss, earth, vegetation. The terrain under foot is more lumpy and uncertain. There are tree roots and broken twigs and clumps of moss. Get the sensation of walking over this rough ground. What sounds can you hear? Are they different sounds from the sounds in the open field? How does it feel to be in the wood? How does it change your mood? Do you walk more slowly? Do you feel more melancholy? Ask yourself these questions and use your imagination and sense memory to explore them.'

When you feel they have thoroughly explored these sensations ask them to imagine a different season and a different environment. Continue as follows:

Winter

'Now imagine it is winter and there is snow on the ground. Imagine you are in the countryside walking through the snow. Don't try to demonstrate it, just feel it for yourself. Feel the cold on your face. Feel the warmth of your clothing. Breathe in the fresh clean smell of snow. Hear the silence and stillness that a fall of snow brings to the countryside. Feel your feet silently crunch through the snow. Is it crunchy snow? How high do you have to lift your feet to step forward? How does it feel to kick the snow around? Imagine there are big snowflakes falling through the air. Imagine what they feel like when they land on your nose. What can you see? Imagine you have walked to the edge of a pond or a small lake, and it is frozen over. Take a step onto the ice. It is thick

enough to take your weight. How does it feel to walk on the ice? Stand there for a moment and feel the snow on you face. Feel the ice underfoot. Step forward onto the ice. How does it feel to walk on ice? It's hard but is it slippy? How slippy? How careful do you have to be? Try it out. Explore it for yourself. Walk to the middle of the pond; it's perfectly safe. The ice is thick. Stop in the middle. Imagine what it is like to stand on the ice of a frozen pond in falling snow in the middle of the silent snow covered countryside. Enjoy it. Let your imagination do the work.'

Now ask them to imagine another season. Continue talking them through it as follows:

Spring

'It's spring now. Imagine the birds are singing with the joy of life, and new buds and leaves are on the trees. You are walking on a gravel path beside a fast-flowing river. Imagine that there are trees on the other side of the path, and the smell of the river mingles with the smell of the undergrowth. The sun is warm through your clothes. You can hear the water flowing, and you can sense the movement and life of the river. Imagine you have taken your shoes off, and you are walking down to the edge of the river where the mud is wet and smooth and oozy. Imagine the mud squelches up through your toes as you walk along. It's disgusting and yet it's delicious at the same time. Comforting and tickly between your toes. Squelchy and grey. The water from the river splashes your ankles, and you stand and watch some ducks swimming by. Let your imagination roam. Don't force it, don't try to be clever or creative, just let your memories work. Let your imagination create the world in your mind and let this imaginary world affect how you feel. Feel the optimism of spring and the freshness of new life.'

Finally, complete the four seasons as follows:

Summer

'It's summer now. Holiday time and you are on a beach. An empty beach and a clear blue sky. Walk along and smell the ocean. Smell the hot sand. Hear the waves as they break on the shore. Imagine that you are wearing only a swimming costume and that the sun is hot on your skin. Maybe there is the smell of suntan lotion and the oily feel of it on your skin. Maybe the sweat is

rolling down your body. Imagine how it feels as the breeze tries to cool your body and the sweat rolls down your tummy. Walk across the beach. Don't force your 'acting'. Don't demonstrate. Imagine that the beach is covered in pebbles and you are not wearing any shoes. How does that feel as you walk towards the water? Try it. See how the pebbles affect the way you walk. Then the patch of pebbles ends, and there is a patch of sand. Hot sand. Hot under your bare feet. Burning. Walk across the hot sand to the water's edge. How do you step? How does the hot sand make your feet feel? Arrive at the edge of the beach where the sand is wet and cooled by the ocean. Stand in the cool wet sand. Imagine the sea as the waves wet your toes and roll round your ankles. Look at the horizon. It's a beautiful day and the meeting of the sea and sky is blurred by haze. The sea is blue, and the waves are breaking on the shore. Feel the heat. Smell the sea. Imagine the whole experience. Imagine you are there looking out to sea. Don't do anything. Just be there.'

As you talk, remind them that they should never try to demonstrate anything. They should just try to feel the sensations for themselves and behave in a natural way. It's important at this stage to eliminate any sense of 'performing' and encourage a sense of 'being'.

RATIONALE   *This exercise uses the improvisers' memory of sensory experiences in order to stimulate their imagination, but at the same time it is being used to prepare them for the next exercise and ultimately the group improvisation called 'The Raft'. By the time you have talked them through the four seasons, their minds will be fully engaged in imaginary experiences, and they will be mentally prepared for their first truthful improvisation. Although the next exercise is written as a new section, there should be no pause, interruption or break of concentration as you continue to talk them through it.*

Preparation for 'The Raft'

With everyone working at the same time, but each person working on their own, the basis of this improvisation is to try to experience what it feels like to be lost at sea on a raft. The water is almost gone. There is a little food. They hear a rescue plane or a helicopter approach. (You can make the noise for them by drumming your fingers on a chair.) The rescue plane doesn't see them and it flies away. Each person should try to experience how it feels to be abandoned.

As I said above, this should be a continuation of the exercise 'Walking on Different Surfaces' so having got them to the point where they are standing on the beach looking out to sea, I usually carry on talking them through like this:

'Now take a step into the sea and feel the water round your calves. Feel the sand beneath your feet and feel the way the waves rush round your legs. Take another step. Go in up to your thighs and start to feel the strength of the ocean as it pulls and pushes your legs. The next wave swells up around your waist, and even as you rise up on your toes, you can't get high enough out of the water to avoid the slight chill that takes your breath away. Go on. Step further into the ocean and feel the water up around your chest. Feel the ocean start to take your weight. Feel the waves move you back and forth as your body partially floats. In you go. Up to your shoulders. The sea lifts you up and lowers you back down so your toes can just touch the bottom. Feel the weight of the sea. The strength of the sea. Let it lift you up, and move you around. Up along, down and back. The coolness of the sea. The sun on your head. Give yourself up to the movement of the sea. Lift and float. Let the strength and movement and flow of the water move you around.'

By now their imaginations should be feeling the power of the ocean and their bodies should be moving as if the waves were lifting them up, pushing them down and moving them around. (If they seem to be holding back from a complete exploration of this experience, I usually join in as I talk, and move around as if my body was being lifted, dropped and shifted by the waves.)

Having established the power of the ocean and the way it can move the body around, you can now use that to help them feel the experience of being on a raft.

With everyone still working on their own, I continue like this:

'Now take a step with your imagination and, still letting the power of the ocean move you as it will, imagine that you are now standing on a small raft that is floating on the water. Feel how the waves move the raft around and how the raft feels beneath your feet. Get your balance. Feel the power. Now imagine that you are on that raft in the middle of the ocean and wherever you look there is just the sea. No land is in sight. The sun is hot on your body. The swell moves you up and down.

'You have been on the raft for two days. You don't know where you are. You have been shipwrecked and although you have food and water with you, you have no idea what will happen next.'

I gradually leave longer gaps between sentences so they can just 'be' in the experience:

'Where are you? What are you thinking?'

'Explore these feelings for yourself.'

'Explore it. Make it as real as you can.'

'You are on your own.'

'On your own.'

. . .

'Hot.'

. . .

'Lonely.'

. . .

. . .

Then I will start to drum lightly on a chair as I continue:

(Clutter-clutter-clutter)

'It's an aeroplane.'

(Clutter-clutter-clutter-clutter-clutter . . .)

'What do you do?'

(Clutter-clutter-clutter . . .)

. . .

'What do you do?'

'Do what you think you would do.'

'Explore your reaction.'

They will usually stand up and start waving; however, they have been going through the various experiences in silence for quite a long time, so they often feel inhibited about vocalising anything. If that is the case I usually yell out 'Help!' to get them started. (In the same way that I moved as if the sea was moving me, this gives them 'permission' to be bold. At this stage they can be rather cautious about being the first to do something new.) I usually leave them feeling lonely and abandoned for a few minutes, and then move straight into the following group improvisation.

Improvisations

The Raft

Having talked them through the previous exercise where each person has been working on their own, they should now be asked to repeat the scenario as if they were all on the same raft and they had all been shipwrecked together. Once you have set this up, they should be allowed to explore this group improvisation without interruption. At some point you can make a rat-a-tat noise to see how they react as a group to the rescue plane, but basically you can keep quiet and just let them improvise. I usually carry straight on from the previous exercise by saying something like:

'Don't lose the world you have created with your imagination. Keep feeling that you are on a raft, but now I want you all to be on the same raft, so will everyone move into the middle of the room and get closer to each other. Imagine you are all on the same raft. Imagine that you are whoever you are. Imagine you know each other just as much as you really do know each other. Imagine you were all shipwrecked together two days ago. What do you do? What happens next?'

(*Pause*)

'What happens next?'

> *(Pause)*

'Explore it.'

> *(Longer pause)*

'Don't rush. Don't force it. Don't demonstrate. Don't try to be the best!! Just see what happens next and do what you think you would do. Work together. Work on your own. See what happens.'

> *(Pause)*

'Keep your imagination working and keep exploring.'

They should now be allowed to improvise on their own with no external input. I usually just slowly circle the group, silently watching what they do. They may not say much for a while, but that doesn't matter. Someone will soon start things off.

This improvisation can now go on for a long time. Twenty to thirty minutes. At some point during that time, you can rat-a-tat-tat on a chair. They'll all know that the sound is a potential rescue plane.

When it is finished, there should be an extended feedback session to allow everyone to talk about the experience.

RATIONALE   *Anything can happen during this improvisation. Sometimes there will be drama. Deaths. Sharks. Deserted islands. Sometimes very little will happen. Some people will just continue to feel things and imagine things and do nothing at all but lie there. Some people will want to take control. Some people will make jokes. Some people will chat quietly in pairs. But the important thing is to let them get on with it without interrupting.*

An improvisation like this helps the improvisers discover what they would do in an unfamiliar situation by experiencing it through their imaginations.

That is what this form of improvisation is for.

As I said, it works best if you go through the 'Walking on Different Surfaces' exercise first, follow it with 'Preparation for "The Raft"' to give them an outline of the scenario, and in order to get their imaginations working fully; then let that exercise flow into 'The Raft' improvisation without any break. In that way they are fully immersed in their own imaginations by the time they are working together.

Session Debriefing

After the improvisation, allow everyone to talk about it. Let them say how they felt. Which moments worked for them and which didn't? It's important that they know that even if people appeared to do nothing at all, they were still improvising correctly providing they stayed true to the scenario. It's important that they know that those people who made drama happen were also improvising correctly. The only thing that they could have done wrong would have been to step out of the improvisation or to not take it seriously. Those people who made jokes on the raft could well have made jokes if they were on a raft in real life. Anything is correct as long as they remain true to the situation.

Most people have never been shipwrecked. Let them know that the exploration of a particular scenario using only their imagination is the essence of this sort of improvisation. It's not a question of discussing and intellectualising how one would behave, it's a question of immersing themselves in the reality of the situation and then letting their natural behaviour take over.

For the group, the important thing is that they have started to work together. They will begin to appreciate each other's differences and they will realise that they can learn from one another.

In short: they will all have started to trust each other a little more.

3

Being There

Have you ever noticed that some people always seem to be at the centre of things while others are always looking to find the centre but never can? And the people at the centre are *always* at the centre, it doesn't matter where they are or what they are doing. And then, wherever they are and whatever they are doing, they always draw other people into their world. And these other people who are looking to be part of someone else's world immediately start worrying that somewhere else might be a better place to be. The grass could be greener, they think.

What is it that the centred people have that makes them content and yet excited by whatever world surrounds them? And why doesn't everyone feel that way?

In 1979 Peter Sellers starred in a film version of a Jerzy Kosinski novel called *Being There*. The main character, Chance, is a gardener who has been isolated from the everyday world. He has not met many people and as a result lives in a world of his own: his garden. When eventually he is forced to leave his garden and go out into the real world, he trusts everyone he meets because he has never encountered sarcasm, metaphor, irony, hyperbole, or any of the other tricks of rhetoric that people use all the time without even thinking about it. Chance is not at all stupid, he just doesn't recognise these rhetorical games. He takes everything that is said at face value. Even the advertisements on television which, up until he leaves his garden, are the only real contact he has had with the outside world. Similarly, he doesn't use rhetoric himself. He is totally honest and direct when he speaks and because the rest of the world is so used to metaphor and simile, his directness is misinterpreted, and he is considered an enigmatic genius. When Chauncey Gardiner (as Chance the Gardener is mistakenly called) talks about the best way to grow roses, people take it as a metaphor for the way to run the country, and he becomes an adviser to the president.

PRESIDENT   Do you think we can stimulate growth through temporary incentives?

CHANCE   As long as the roots are not severed . . . all is well . . . There will be growth in the spring.

Jerzy Kosinski called his novel *Being There* because his main protagonist, Chance, is entirely in the centre of his own world. He is 'in the moment'. And his is a world without deception. A rose is a rose is a rose, and that's it. If Chance is talking about roses then he is talking about roses, not people, not towns and cities, not the economy, not even flowers in general. Just roses. He is not trying to impress. He is not trying to entertain. He is just 'being there'. He is centred and consequently he draws the people around him into his world.

Explorative Improvisation

IF I HAD TO ISOLATE ONE THING THAT IS VITAL FOR AN improviser to master, it would have to be the ability to 'be there'. It's the main skill. If you trust yourself, trust your partner and believe in the world you create together, you don't have to 'do' anything, you just have to 'be'.

The problem with 'being there' for an improviser is that someone is usually watching them improvise, and as soon as any performer feels they are being watched, they want to put on a show. And it's that desire to 'put on a show' that promotes the desire to entertain. The trouble is that once an improviser starts to entertain an audience, even an audience of one, the ability to be 'in the moment' and behave truthfully becomes a problem, because part of the brain is focused on the audience reaction and how to manipulate it.

Of course, experienced actors continually juggle with the truth/entertainment paradox along with all the other mental and physical skills they employ during a performance, but when improvisation is used in rehearsals as an exploration tool, the desire to entertain the director or the other actors can only be a distraction.

For inexperienced improvisers it is even harder to ignore the observers. It's very difficult to act normally when people are looking at you, because you feel you ought to 'do' something. Ask anyone who has had to walk through an auditorium to accept a diploma, or walk across a dance floor to ask someone for a dance. Even the simple, everyday act of walking becomes a problem when you feel you are being watched. It makes you self-conscious and awkward. Think about the way people behave when you want to take a photograph of them. They pull funny faces. They assume heroic poses. They jump around. The fact is that when people realise they are being observed and the pressure is on, they want to do something. And they want to be liked.

And the easiest way to be sure that people like you is to make them laugh. Laughter is a physical/aural manifestation that everything is alright. If the audience laugh, then they must like you. Consequently, inexperienced improvisers often want, above all, to make people laugh. Of course laughter is a fantastic reaction to an improvised *performance*. As are other reactions that are not so easy for the performer to hear, such as anxiety, fear, compassion, apprehension, and love, etc. etc. And a skilful improvised performance can take an audience on quite a complex emotional journey. But in *explorative* improvisation, audience laughter, audience tears, audience sighs are all a distraction. As is the desire to promote them. The improviser must strive to think and behave as if the 'audience' (the director and the other actors) were not there.

They must forget about trying to entertain. They must forget about being liked. And, above all, they must not be afraid of being boring. They must just 'be there'.

For without that sense of unobserved 'truth', there can be no proper exploration of situation, character or relationships. And ultimately very little will be discovered that can be of use as a rehearsal tool. *And the whole point of explorative improvisation is to experience and discover things outside the scripted life of a character or a play.*

Exercises

What Animal I'd Like to Be

Ask everyone to sit in a circle. One at a time each person tells the rest of the group what animal they would most like to be and why. They can talk for as long as they like, but they tend to keep it quite short. (i.e. 'I'd like to be a lion because they are so proud.' Or 'I'd like to be an eagle and fly over the mountains looking at the world below.')

RATIONALE   *This is simply to get people talking about things and using their imagination.*

Who I'd Like to Meet

Ask everyone to sit in a circle. One at a time each person tells the rest of the group who they would most like to meet and why they would like to meet them. Tell them that each person has to talk for one minute. (In order to take the pressure off them, I will often divide the group in half and set up two circles, so that no one is ever the only person in the room talking.)

RATIONALE   *This exercise is to develop their ability to talk in front of a large group of people using their own words and expressing their own ideas. For some of them a minute is absolutely no problem at all, but for others it seems like an eternity and they run out of things to say. However, if you encourage them to choose someone to 'meet' that they know a lot about, that helps the more reticent members of the group.*

⚑ The Lottery

With the whole group working at the same time, but with each person working on their own, talk them through a solo improvisation about winning the lottery. They should be trying to find the truth of the situation for themselves and although they are not being asked to 'mime' their reactions, they would obviously do most of this in silence because there is no one else to talk to. I usually say something like the following:

'Imagine you are walking home at the end of the day. It is winter, so it is already dark, and it is drizzling rain. Don't demonstrate, just walk. Just believe in it and try to think the thoughts you might think on an occasion like this. Imagine how you would feel. You are getting close to home. Imagine you are walking down your street and you arrive at your own front door. Let yourself in exactly the way you would really let yourself in, and then do the sort of thing you would do next. Imagine that you live on your own, or that there is no one else there, so you are completely unobserved. Where would you put your coat? Would you have to put on any heating? Would you make yourself a cup of tea? Imagine what you would do and then do it. But also, whatever else you are doing, put on the television so it's playing in the background. You vaguely watch it. It's showing a programme where ordinary people pretend to be stars. They get dressed up like a famous person and try to sing a song so they sound just like that person. Imagine someone is on television trying to sound and look like Britney Spears (or whoever is popular at the moment). You watch for a minute. Then you realise that it is a friend of yours! It's someone you were at school with who is now pretending to be Britney Spears . . . How do you react? What do you do? Don't feel you have to demonstrate your reaction, just do what you would do. Let your imagination take control and try to react truthfully.

'After a while, flick channels and imagine that the lottery draw comes on. Imagine that you buy a lottery ticket each week so you are mildly interested. The first number that comes up is 19. Your mother's birthday. Each week you always use that number for luck so there is a minor thrill of excitement and you wonder where you put the ticket. The next number comes up. '13.' Yes. Unlucky for some so you chose it to be perverse. The thrill of excitement grows and you start to look for the ticket, but can't find it. Is it in your coat pocket? Did you put it in the kitchen drawer? '24!' Was it 24 or 26 you put down? You can't remember. Where is that damn ticket? Is it in your wallet? '7.' No idea. But here's the ticket! You've found it, and yes, you did choose 24. And, and,

and, and . . . YES! 7! That's 19, 13, 24 and 7. You've got four out of six right. There's bound to be money in that. '8.' Before you have time to even think you get the fifth number right. How do you feel? What do you do? Don't demonstrate, just feel it. Imagine it. There's only one more number you need and it's a 31. 'Come on. Come on.' You think to yourself, 'Come on, 31. Come!' The balls jump around. One of them bounces up the funnel and . . . YES! It's '31'! . . . All six numbers are correct! You've won the lottery!!!'

You can build the excitement of the lottery numbers by the way you use your voice. It will help them feel the excitement for themselves. As soon as you tell them that they have won the lottery, stop speaking and let them do whatever they do. Let them carry on for five minutes or so and then bring the exercise to an end.

RATIONALE   *The purpose of this exercise is to get them used to the idea of improvising truthfully without feeling the need to talk. It's relatively easy for them to behave realistically when they are asked to recreate a familiar experience like walking home or making tea. So once that is established, they will be prepared to continue with a realistic solo improvisation when an unfamiliar experience is introduced: like seeing a friend on television; or winning the lottery.*

DEBRIEFING   *After the exercise is over, allow them to discuss the experience together. Has anyone won the lottery? Did they feel they behaved truthfully? Let them know that whatever they did was right as long as they stayed truthful to the exploration. Different people react differently in any situation. Also explain that although most of the improvisation was talked through in detail, it went on for a few minutes after the moment of exhilaration or triumph with no more instructions. That was for two reasons. One, because life goes on even after moments of exhilaration and triumph, and it's always interesting to discover what happens next: what happens after the climax can sometimes be more interesting than the climax. And secondly, because it helps them to understand that they need to continue to concentrate and explore even when an improvisation appears to have finished.*

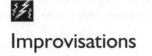

Improvisations

Minimal-Word Group Improvisations

Divide the group into two halves. Let one half be the audience for the other. The first half does a group improvisation of a doctor's waiting room for about ten minutes while the other group watches. Then the second half does a group improvisation of a queue of people waiting in line to see a smash-hit movie while the first half watches.

RATIONALE   *This exercise is to introduce them to the concept of just being truthful, without having to 'do' anything.*

DEBRIEFING   *Discuss how real these improvisations appeared. Ten to one there will have been a lot of drama and action. Ask them to compare these improvisations to their own real experience of situations like these. Let them know that the reality is more important than the drama at this stage of the training. Reinforce the message that they are not expected to be interesting! They just have to be truthful to the situation.*

Minimal-Word Improvisations

Ask the group to divide themselves into pairs. With the rest of the group watching, give each pair an improvisation where there would normally be no speaking. Before they start, explain that they must really think about the situation they are in. If, for instance, they are supposed to be studying in a library, they must really imagine what they are studying. They must imagine what book they are reading. If they imagine that they are writing an essay, they must imagine the words they write down; imagine the pen they are using; and the paper they are writing on. They could also imagine that they are not allowed to speak or to disturb anyone.

Tell them that during the first part of the improvisation they must think of something they really want to say to the other person, but tell them they can't say it until they get a signal. In that way the desire to speak will build. (I usually give the signal after about three minutes by clapping my hands.)

Here are some suggestions for Minimal-Word Improvisations:

- *Strangers sheltering from the rain*

- *Strangers in a café*

- *Strangers waiting to take an exam*

- *Strangers waiting for a bus*

- *Strangers sitting next to each other on a bus*

- *Strangers in an art gallery*

- *Strangers sunbathing*

- *Strangers at a funeral*

- *Strangers studying in a library*

- *People listening to a new CD together for the first time*

- *Strangers watching a game of chess*

- *Strangers sitting in a cathedral*

RATIONALE   *This exercise is to give them the opportunity to put the concept of 'being there' into action. Although it is hard for them to do very little, they start to learn that 'less can be more' in the search for truth in an improvisation. It also helps them practise the desire to communicate. When we speak to other people it is because we want to communicate with them. So often in an improvisation people speak because they think they ought to, not because they have something to say.*

DEBRIEFING   *After each improvisation discuss what was truthful. Point out whatever seemed to be moments of demonstration. Encourage moments of silence and stillness. They don't have to force the issue, they just have to behave realistically. And they don't have to speak unless they've got something to say.*

Session Debriefing

At the end of the class discuss the ability to do nothing in front of an audience. Ask them how easy or difficult they found it. Really make them understand that, if it is truthful to do nothing, then nothing is what they must do.

There are two dangers that crop up with inexperienced improvisers, and they are the oral extremes. One is the improviser who doesn't know what to say, and the other is the improviser who can't stop talking. Both of these extremes are brought about by fear and the feeling of being in the spotlight. If they learn to forget that someone might be watching and just find the truth of a situation, then the words that come out of their mouths will be the words they would use in real life. That is all they have to do in an improvisation.

They just have to 'be there'.

4

Atmospheres

A lot of the time we take the atmosphere of a place for granted. We don't even notice it because we expect it to be like that. Walk into a busy pub and you expect it to be lively. Sit alone on the rocks by a stormy sea and of course you feel the power of nature and the insignificance of mankind. A funeral feels like a funeral. A romantic evening feels like a romantic evening. In fact, the only time we really become aware that there is an atmosphere around us is when it changes. When someone or something 'breaks' the atmosphere.

Funnily enough I sometimes used to drink in a pub near a theatre, even though I wasn't working in that theatre. It was always a lively place before a show because it would be full of people who had come from out of town by coach. Everyone would be jabbering away in excited anticipation of a good night out. One evening I walked into the pub and there was an extraordinary change in the atmosphere. It was just as full of people as usual and the people were just as excited about a night out. If anything they were even more animated than usual, but the atmosphere was entirely different. And what was the difference? The difference was the sound. It was very quiet. Hardly any noise at all. And the reason it was so quiet was that the people in the pub were all deaf and they were jabbering away using only their hands. Signing.

Pubs and restaurants often try to create a 'good atmosphere' with lighting and music. Low lighting creates an intimate atmosphere. Familiar music creates a friendly atmosphere. Classical music creates a sophisticated atmosphere. Atmosphere is around us all the time, and we hardly notice it until it goes wrong.

One year I drove round Italy on my motorbike for five weeks. I was camping, I was on my own, and I was completely self-contained. It was a journey into my soul. It rained all through France, which is pretty depressing on a motorbike and massively depressing when you are camping. Imagine it. You're out in the rain all day. You get to a campsite and the campsite is partially flooded. You unroll the tent – which is still wet from yesterday – onto the wet ground. You set it up in a place that avoids as many puddles as possible. You get into the tent with your motorcycling wetsuit still on, and you try to remove your wet clothes in a space that's smaller than your average toilet and only about three feet high. Then you try to cook without setting the tent on fire. It's not a lot of fun. The next day it's still raining, and you have to pack up and set off for another day of motorcycling in the rain. It was all very gloomy.

I can't remember how long it took to get to Italy. Four days perhaps. But as I emerged from a tunnel through the Alps the atmosphere was completely different. The sun was shining and my spirits lifted.

Nevertheless, I was on my own, and I didn't speak French, Italian, German, or any language except English. Pathetic, I know, and I'm ashamed of it, but that's my problem. One day I will . . . One day.

I'd never been to Italy before, but I knew that it was famous for Art. So in order to plan some sort of route before I embarked on the trip, I had asked an artist friend of mine where he thought I should go and what he thought I should look out for. He'd given me good advice. He'd said, 'Why don't you focus on Piero della Francesca and Giotto. A lot of their paintings are frescos: painted straight onto the walls and ceilings. And because it is hard to move a wall into an art gallery, you have to travel to see their paintings in situ. You could plan a whole route travelling from church to church.' A good idea, I thought. So before I went I bought some art books and a map and I planned my journey.

It was extraordinary to drive fifty miles into the middle of nowhere to find a church with only one painting in it. I particularly remember seeing 'The Pregnant Madonna' by Piero della Francesca. You could hardly believe that such an important and precious work of art is just there, on the end wall of a tiny church in the middle of rural Italy, unguarded and unprotected.

The experience is unsettling.*

The first time you see Assisi it can't fail to impress. The route that I took had me approaching it across a plain and from miles off you can see the Basilica di San Francesco clinging to the steep edge of Mount Asi. I'll never forget that first sighting.

I had a good time in Assisi, looking at the fabulous paintings of Giotto in the Basilica and strolling around the shops full of Francis of Assisi sandals and religious icons. In fact, I became rather obsessed with Francis during my stay there, reading his life story (and later on trekking through the mountains to find La Verna where he received the stigmata). So while I was in Assisi I had to visit La Porziuncola where he had lived. This is a tiny chapel on the plain outside Assisi. It's not much bigger than a garden shed, but it's easy to find because they have built an enormous church over it and around it called the Basilica di Santa Maria degli Angeli (the Basilica of Saint Mary of the Angels).

It was a really hot day when I visited. I drove down from Assisi, parked my bike and went in search of an ice cream. The tourists were milling around; the teenagers were zipping about amongst them on their scooters; and the stalls and kiosks were doing a roaring trade in tourist guides, ice creams, pizzas and water. Anything and everything that could make them a few lire. It was very hot and the sunshine was very bright. It was noisy. People were shouting and laughing. There was lots of hustle and bustle, and I felt that relaxed confusion you get when you are on holiday in a hot country.

Eventually I decided to go to see La Porziuncola and headed for the entrance of the Basilica. And here's the point. As I stepped inside, everything changed. After the brightness of the sunshine it was so dark I could hardly see. After the midday heat it was cool. Cool. After the bustle of the crowd it was calm and hushed. After the noise of the tourists there was cathedral silence punctuated only by the melancholy sound of an organ coming from somewhere in the musky, shadowy depths. The air was cool to breathe and laced with the smell of incense. When people spoke they spoke in hushed, respectful whispers.

The whole atmosphere had changed, and the way people behaved and spoke changed with it.

After taking a look at Saint Francis's little church and letting my imagination roam at will, filling the little shed with animals and birds and

---

* I revisited this painting in 2006 and amazingly enough, they *have* moved the wall! The little church is locked and devoid of art and the picture has been carefully taken away and restored, and is on display in a small museum nearby. Things change.

Saint Francis himself, I stepped outside the Basilica once again. Back to the heat. Back to the noise. Back to the smell of pizza. Back to the blinding sunshine. Back to the shouting. Back to the entirely different atmosphere of bustling tourism.

Analysing Atmosphere

WHATEVER WE ARE DOING, THERE IS ALWAYS AN ATMOS-phere around us, and these different atmospheres affect our behaviour. But the funny thing is, people in an improvisation usually just accept the atmosphere of the room they are improvising in and go with that.

However, if improvisers are able to imagine that they are in a different place and they allow their imagination to create the atmosphere, then they will be able to make the place come alive for themselves, affecting the way they move and talk. It will even affect what they say and how they think.

So in order to explore this and use it in an improvisation, it is important for improvisers to analyse various atmospheres and register the impact that these atmospheres have on their behaviour.

Exercises

Soundscapes

Divide the group into two halves. Each half has to decide on a place that has a particular atmosphere but also has a mixture of sounds – a factory, a fairground, the jungle, etc. (If possible each group should work in a separate room so the other group doesn't know what they are working on.) Then each group has to recreate the sounds of the environment they have chosen. Although it is acceptable to use props to make noises, the more the soundscape can be created using their own voices and bodies, the better. It's also best to keep spoken words out of this unless they are indistinct and in the distance. Subtlety is good. Tiny sounds and noises work well. When each group feels they have created an acceptable soundscape, then one group should lie on the floor with their eyes shut and the other group should 'perform' their soundscape around them, seeing how realistic they can make the atmosphere. The group lying on the floor should be able to guess where the soundscape is supposed to be.

When one group has done this, the other should have a go.

RATIONALE   *This exercise gets people working together as a group, negotiating their ideas, and learning from each other. But it is also a good exploration of atmosphere because the soundscapes really do conjure up the feeling of a particular environment for the people who are lying on the floor and listening.*

A Place I Know

With each person working on their own, but with everyone working at the same time, ask them all to sit comfortably, shut their eyes, and think of somewhere that they know well and that has a particular atmosphere. It could be their bedroom, it could be a fairground that they used to visit when they were children, it could be a club they visited last night, but it's important that it is a place they can remember quite clearly. Then ask them to use their senses to isolate various aspects of the atmosphere. I usually talk them through this in the following way:

'What can you hear? Is it quiet or is it noisy? What noises are close to you – the sound of your own breathing, the ticking of a clock? And what sounds are in the distance – dogs barking in the street, wind in the trees, falling rain? Also think of the sounds in between – someone cooking downstairs and clattering pots and pans, traffic outside an open window, music in the background. When you have identified these sounds, start thinking about what you can smell. Can you smell the cooking downstairs? Can you smell the ocean or the cut grass? Is there a sweet fresh smell where you are or is it musky and damp? Is there a smell of incense or perfume? Smoke or hot coals? Does the smell leave a taste in your mouth? Does it make you happy, sad, frightened or calm? What atmosphere does the smell evoke?

'Now think about how you feel physically. Are you warm or cold? Is there a breeze or is the air still? Are you sitting in a comfortable place surrounded by cushions or are you on a hard wooden bench? Are you bundled up in warm clothes or does the sun burn your skin? How does the surrounding world affect you physically?

'Lastly, think about what you can see. Keep you eyes closed and try to imagine every detail of the place you are recreating in your mind. Is it bright or is it gloomy? Can you see lots of colours or is the general aspect pale and washed out? What details can you see in your imagination? Try to remember everything. The colour of the walls, the carpet, the furniture. What is on the shelves? What is outside the window? Is the place you are in lit by electricity or by the sun? Can you see other people? Can you see animals? Think of all the details. Remember all the colours. Remember how the shadows fall.'

When they are fully immersed in their imaginations, you can tell them that you are going to ask them individually to describe the place they are 'in'. As you talk to each person, it's best to get close to them, and to ask your questions quietly. They should keep their eyes shut, continue to imagine they are in their particular place, and then just answer the questions.

When you have finished with the first person, he or she can then become a 'questioner' and each of you can go and talk to a new person. When you have finished questioning the new people, they too can become 'questioners' and so on.

RATIONALE   *This exercise is to get people to think of the details of a place they are imagining, and to explore how the atmosphere impacts on their senses. As they do it, they will discover that the memory of the place affects their thoughts and behaviour.*

DEBRIEFING   *Discuss what happened during this exercise. Was it easy to 'feel' the atmosphere of the places they were imagining? Did the atmosphere slow them down and make them calm, or did it excite them and make them want to move around? Did it affect the way they answered the questions? Did it affect the way they thought or the way they talked?*

Exploring Atmosphere

This exercise is based on my experience in Assisi as described above.

With each person working on their own, but with everyone working at the same time, talk the group through the change of atmosphere from outside to inside a much-visited Italian cathedral. Before you start, describe the layout of the room you are working in, so they know exactly what part of that room represents the outside world, what part represents the cathedral doors, and what part represents the interior of the cathedral. Start off describing all the detail of a hot busy Italian street, going through the senses. The heat of the sun on their bodies. The sound of Italian conversations, busy traffic and scooters buzzing past. The smell of pizzas cooking nearby. The brightness of the sun and the colour of the sky, etc. And then ask them to walk into the cathedral and feel the change of atmosphere. Again, using sensory experience, describe the dark, gloomy interior. The quiet stillness. The smell of incense. The hushed sound of an organ playing somewhere, etc. When they have experienced the atmosphere of the cathedral interior have them walk out into the bright sunshine, again describing the change of atmosphere. The blinding sunlight. The hustle and bustle of a city, etc. When they are all 'outside' get them to imagine that they can see an old barn outside the cathedral which has a spiritual significance. Tell them it was used by Saint Francis to keep his animals in. They can take photographs of it but they can't get close because it is across the other side of a river. Also the sun is so bright after the gloom of the cathedral that they can hardly see the barn at all.

Improvisations

Cathedral

This group improvisation should follow on from the exercise above. Tell them that they are going to go through the whole sequence again, but this time it will be a group improvisation. They are to be a group of tourists who are sightseeing together. Tell them they have to stay together as a group and also tell them that you won't be talking them through the improvisation this time, but they should just follow the sequence. Of course, they can now chat as they go. Get them started and then let them explore the scenario in their own time.

The improvisation can stop when they see the barn across the other side of the river, but if the group is quite accomplished, you can continue without a break by adding the 'Virgin Mary' improvisation described below.

RATIONALE   *They now know how to explore atmosphere through its impact on their senses, so this is a chance for them to use that in conjunction with a proper improvisation, where the changes of atmosphere are supporting – rather than dominating – an improvisation.*

🖊 Virgin Mary

This is a continuation of the 'Cathedral' improvisation and can be added without a break. However, it is quite a bold step into unexplored territory and should be used with caution.

When they eventually come out of the cathedral as a group and see the barn across the river I usually say, 'As you squint your eyes in the blinding sunlight, you see a vision of the Virgin Mary rising above the roof of the barn.' See how they react!

RATIONALE   *In a way it is a bit of a trick to add that to the end when they don't expect it, because they don't know how to react. Often they will just stare blankly and wait to see what everyone else does or they will say things like 'I wonder how they do that?' or 'It must be a trick.' But although it's not an exploration of atmosphere, it's an important part of the improvisation training. First of all, it teaches them that they must get used to staying in the moment – staying in the improvisation – whatever happens or whatever is thrown at them. This is rather like the moment in* Midnight Cowboy *that I described in the Introduction when Dustin Hoffman unexpectedly has to dodge a yellow cab and carries on acting while he incorporates the interruption into the scene. It's that sort of concentration and commitment that needs to be encouraged.*

But secondly, the moment with the vision of the Virgin Mary is to encourage the improvisers to be adventurous and dangerous. By saying, 'I wonder how they do that,' they are opting out of a challenging reaction. Of course it's legitimate to respond in that way, but surely it is more interesting to behave as if they are having a real spiritual experience or a frightening experience or a confusing experience. Remember I said, 'You see a vision of the Virgin Mary rising above the roof of the barn,' not 'It looks like there is . . . ' or 'It seems as if there is . . . ' or 'You think you see . . . ' I said the absolute positive, 'You see . . . ', so they have to learn to react literally as if it is happening and there is a vision. And if it did happen what would they do? Fall on their knees and pray? Start babbling in tongues? Faint? Scream? Cry with joy? Surely all these are more interesting reactions than assuming it is all done with mirrors.

Of course it's hard to expect them to react that way at this stage of the training, especially when there has been such a strong emphasis on reality. But as actors and improvisers, they may eventually have to find the truth behind some very extraordinary scenarios: an alien in a spaceship, a pig that talks, an invisible man, etc.

But basically, the 'Virgin Mary' add-on is to teach them to take risks and to be unafraid of truthful extremes.

DEBRIEFING   *Let them talk about the experience, the changes of atmosphere and how they felt during the group improvisation. And then talk about their reaction to the vision of the Virgin Mary. Explain the points discussed in the rationale above so they realise that they can be bold and extreme as long as they stay truthful and realistic.*

⚡ Places with Atmosphere

Ask the group to divide themselves into pairs and ask each pair to decide on a relationship. They should be people who know each other quite well, like best friends or brother and sister. And then get them to improvise a very simple conversation around a bland subject. Their favourite food or what they like to watch on television or which film star they fancy. The sort of conversation that they could have anywhere and is not dictated by the environment they are in. All the pairs can do this at the same time, since there is absolutely no need to watch these conversations. They are like a rehearsal.

Next, give each pair an environment with a particular atmosphere and get them to have the same conversation, but let it take place in this new environment. They must stick more or less to the conversation they had before, and they should not start referring to the place they are in. This time the rest of the group can watch each improvisation and if the environments are handed out secretly, it's quite good fun for the audience to try to guess where the improvisation is supposed to be taking place.

Here are some suggestions for environments:

- *A church*

- *A busy pub*

- *A prison cell (which the pair have shared for four months)*

- *A wedding reception*

- *A get-together after a funeral*

- *A very hot beach*

- *At home waiting for the World Cup to begin on television*

- *Lost in the woods*

- *Waiting to take an exam*

- *The morning after the night before (both with hangovers)*

For this exercise it's quite easy to imagine the whispery atmosphere of a church or the headache of a hangover; but it's hard for two people to get the sense of a noisy pub, where they would have to shout at each other and be continually jostled by the crowd, when they are on their own and there is no crowd. It's also hard to really experience the sense of boredom and never-ending time in a prison cell; as is the heat exhaustion of a beach where every word is an effort to speak. Get them to explore these extremes. If they are having difficulties, ask the rest of the group to create the atmosphere around them and let them try again. If everyone is creating the atmosphere of a noisy pub, for instance, then the improvisers will find it easier to shout and be jostled. If the group recreates the soundscape of the beach, it's easier for the improvisers to imagine the heat and exhaustion.

RATIONALE   *These improvisations are to give them the opportunity to put the exploration of atmosphere into practice. But also, by allowing them to see other people doing these improvisations, it helps them to understand how a particular atmosphere can affect a scenario.*

Session Debriefing

After all these exercises, let them discuss how an environment can alter the way people speak and behave. Then remind them about the other important lesson that they should learn – that they can be courageous and bold in their explorations and choices and still maintain a truthful improvisation.

Remind them, yet again, that these improvisations are not 'to get things right,' but to explore character, relationships and experiences and to see what happens.

There is no right or wrong, there is only exploration and discovery.

5

Adjusting the Scenario

There are those that obey the rules and those that break the rules. Interestingly enough, even though rules are created to help make things work, the people who break them are often more admired than those who obey them. People who obey rules are often criticised for not having any imagination – 'He just does things by the book' – whereas outlaws like Robin Hood and Al Capone are often admired for their adventurous spirit and derring-do. And they certainly broke the rules.

The rules of law.

There is another category, of course, and that is those people who 'rewrite the rules'. They are also admired. But notice that the expression doesn't say 'They write their own rules,' it says they are 'rewriting' them, so if that is the case then the rules must already exist. And by rewriting the rules, it implies that they are improving them. And that is what we are talking about here. How to rewrite the rules, or, in the case of improvisation, how to adjust the scenario.

When nineteen-year-old Robert Zimmerman decided to stop trying to sound like Little Richard and began to sing like Woody Guthrie, he wasn't exactly breaking the rules of pop music, but he was 'adjusting the scenario' to suit himself.

Here are some of the rules of the time:

As a young singer hoping to have a career in music you needed to:

a) Listen to lots of up-to-date popular music and get to know the latest trend.

b) Play in public to get experience and confidence.

c) See if you could get work performing with established musicians.

d) Go to a big city and try to get to know influential people.

e) Change your name so you could have the strength of a made-up personality.

Robert Zimmerman did all those things. He obeyed the rules.

a) He listened to lots of music as a teenager. Blues, country music, rock and roll, etc. If he couldn't get hold of records he was known to steal them to increase his music collection.

b) He played wherever people would have him, first of all at school and then at local dances with his own rock-and-roll band and then later in coffee bars and cellar clubs as the newest trend – folk music – hit the scene.

c) He played in the backing band on a tour of the latest teen heart-throb, Bobby Vee, and later played harmonica on the first album of a Joan Baez soundalike – Carolyn Hester. Joan Baez was established as the queen of the new folk-music movement, and Robert soon got to know her and made numerous appearances as an unbilled newcomer singing duets with her in her stage show,

d) and of course he went to New York and met everybody he could, and

e) changed his name to Bob Dylan.

All this before the age of twenty-one.

But what made him succeed where others failed? Let's face it, there are always hundreds of hopeful singers trying to be popular music stars. Well, Robert/Bob understood the rules – in fact, he knew them very well – but without ignoring them, he made a few adjustments of his own.

This is what he did:

a) He made up a completely fictitious biography.

b) He started singing like an old man.

c) He wrote his own songs.

d) He wrote songs about social injustice and Cold War paranoia.

Other people have fictionalised their former lives, of course, but not quite so outrageously as Robert Zimmerman did when he created a history for Bob Dylan. This middle-class Jewish boy from Minnesota told everyone that he came from Oklahoma and that he had spent his teenage years working in a travelling circus. He told people that he had been taught to play the blues by Southern bluesmen whereas he had, in fact, learned all his songs from records. He made up a complete history for himself which totally eliminated his Mum and Dad and all his school friends. Then, when he was nineteen, he started to copy Woody Guthrie almost like an impersonator. He dressed like Woody, he sang Woody's songs, and he made his voice sound like Woody's (Woody Guthrie was an old man by this time, so Bob Dylan made himself sound like an old man too), and then he started to write songs about social injustice just like Woody had, twenty years earlier.

All this made him the darling of the burgeoning folk-music scene in New York, because they thought he was the real thing. A country hick. A genuine down-home Okie, with a real sense of injustice, playing a battered acoustic guitar. And because of this he became the hero of the civil rights movement. He marched on Washington with Martin Luther King and he played to itinerant farm workers in the Southern states.

Then, as he started to obey the rules of his new folk-singing persona, he wanted to adjust the scenario again. When he was twenty-three and the undoubted king of the folk scene, being totally revered by folk tradition-alists like Pete Seeger, he was invited to play at the highly prestigious Newport Folk Festival. Everyone expected this country boy 'protest singer' to stir their middle-class, self-righteous indignation with songs about oppression and atom bombs, but in fact he burst onto the stage with an electric band and played rock and roll. Yes, he was expected to entertain. Yes, he was expected to make music. Yes, he was expected to sing songs he had written himself, and he was expected to make people think about life. But he wasn't expected to play with an electric band. That wasn't considered to be real folk music. That was pop! Yet again he had adjusted the scenario.

Throughout his life, Bob Dylan always did things that weren't expected of him. He made a country-music album when he was the king of alternative rock. He became a Christian when all his hippy contemporaries were becoming Buddhists, junkies and acid-heads. And he started his never-ending tour, playing over a hundred live gigs a year, year after year, when other successful musicians would hang up their hats and only perform live when they had an album to sell. And then in his mid-sixties he became a disc-jockey with his own radio show, when he surely didn't need the money or the exposure.

He was no outlaw. He obeyed the rules. But *he always adjusted the scenario.*

So how does this apply to an improviser?

Ground Rules and Given Circumstances

ITHINK THE IMPORTANT THING TO UNDERSTAND HERE IS THE difference between 'adjusting the rules' so that unexpected things can happen within a structured framework and 'complete anarchy' when the rules are ignored entirely. Some improvisers think that they are being creative when they break all the rules, try to shock people and do anything at all to get noticed, but that is not the point of this exploration. The point is to work within the ground rules and see how creative you can be without inhibition. I'll be talking more about this in Chapter 13: Releasing the Imagination, but for now there are two important things for improvisers to remember in this context:

1. LISTEN CAREFULLY TO THE GROUND RULES SO YOU UNDERSTAND THE STRUCTURE.

2. DON'T INHIBIT YOUR IMAGINATION BY INVENTING LIMITATIONS THAT AREN'T THERE.

The first point is obvious really, especially when it comes to an improvisation. If, for instance, two people are asked to improvise a scene where 'a brother and a sister are walking down Oxford Street,' it's completely missing the point if one of them begins the improvisation by saying, 'Stop the car, Mum, and look at those lions.' The rules are: 'a brother and a sister' not a mother and son, 'walking' not driving, and 'down Oxford Street' not at the zoo or in Africa. And although Mum could be driving past at the time and a lion could have escaped from the zoo, it's stretching the point so much that they might just as well have been asked to 'do anything you like'. If they completely ignore the structure then the building collapses. Anarchy doesn't help the process of exploration and discovery.

However, after suggesting such an improvisation, I sometimes get asked questions like:

'Is he an older brother?'

'Are they adults?'

'Is this Oxford Street in London?'

'Is it daytime?'

And my answer would have to be 'It could be any of those things. The only ground rules you have to obey are: *a brother and a sister walking down Oxford Street.* Listen to the instructions and don't inhibit your imagination by inventing limitations that aren't there.'

A number of basic rules of improvisation should be obeyed:

1. PRETEND TO BE SOMEONE ELSE.

2. IMAGINE THAT YOU ARE SOMEWHERE ELSE.

3. TALK TO OTHER IMPROVISERS IN A REALISTIC WAY.

Added to that are some particular rules that I ask people to obey:

4. KEEP GOING UNTIL YOU ARE ASKED TO STOP.

5. DON'T TALK TO PEOPLE WHO AREN'T THERE.

6. DON'T TALK ON IMAGINARY TELEPHONES.

7. BE TRUTHFUL.

8. MIME PROPS.

9. DON'T BE ANIMALS.

10. DON'T ALLOW YOURSELF TO GET INTO IMPROVISED ABUSIVE ARGUMENTS.

11. DON'T 'BLOCK'.

12. USE YOUR OWN NAMES.

Finally there are the 'given circumstances,' as it were, which are the details of the particular scenario. And the rules for that are:

13. BE TRUE TO THE SITUATION.

14. BE TRUE TO THE CHARACTER.

The rest is up to the improvisers.

A brother and a sister walking down Oxford Street.

'Yes, you can go into a shop.'

'Yes, it can start raining.'

'Yes, the sister could be 35 and the brother could be 17.'

'Yes, you can lose your wallet.'

'Yes, you can dance down the street singing songs from *The Wizard of Oz*.'

'Yes, you can have a heart attack and die!'

They could do any of those things because no one has said they can't and each of those dramatically truthful choices would fall within the ground rules and the given circumstances.

Thinking Outside the Box

In order to help the improvisers fully understand how to be as inventive as possible, this session takes them on a journey which starts at the opposite end of the creative spectrum. First of all they are asked to make rhythmic sounds and mechanical movements, and although they can choose their own sounds and movements, they all have to work together following a strict automatic rhythm. They then move to an exercise where they have to be parts of a machine: mechanical and automatic. However, these are machines that make things, so they are now starting to be more creative and productive. Finally, I introduce them to ways in which they can become machines that are so artistically creative they are hardly mechanical at all. Then they begin to understand how to 'think outside the box'.

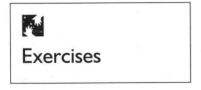

Exercises

Syncopated Sounds

Ask everyone to stand in a circle and set up a rhythm by clicking their fingers in time with a beat of about one second. Once the rhythm is established, ask one person in the circle to make a musical or percuss-ive sound that fits in with the beat of the finger clicking and to keep repeating it. Then ask the next person in the circle to add a different musical or percussive sound and then the next person, all the way round the circle until a complex syncopated rhythm involving everyone is happening. At this point you can ask the whole group to move around the room, weaving in and out of each other, still making their sounds. As they move, they will hear different sounds and rhythms complementing and adding to their own.

Eventually, still making the sounds, ask them to reform the circle and then, starting with the person who did the first sound, stop them one by one until the last person who added their sound is the only one left. (I usually stop each person by standing in front of them and indicating with my hands that they should finish, rather than saying anything to them out loud.)

RATIONALE   *By making their own syncopated, repetitive sounds, they learn to be individually creative, while, at the same time, they work in harmony with the group.*

Rhythmical Moves

Ask everyone to stand in a circle and to set up a rhythm by clicking their fingers in time with a beat of about one second. Once the rhythm is established, ask one person in the circle to make a mechanical movement in time with the rhythm of the finger clicking, and to add a mechanical sound and to keep repeating both. Then ask the next person in the circle to add a different mechanical movement and sound. Then the next person, all the way round the circle until everyone is making sounds and movements like they are bits of machinery. Once they are all going strong, and in rhythm with each other, they can be asked to speed up and slow down.

RATIONALE   *Continuing from the previous exercise, they now add repeti-tive movements. These two exercises prepare them for the following exercise.*

Machines

Divide the group into two halves and ask each half to form a circle. Then one person from each group goes into the middle of their circle and makes a mechanical movement and sound. Once that is established, another person joins the first person and adds another mechanical movement and sound that has to be connected with, or related to, the first person's. Then a third person joins them and then a fourth until everyone in each group is part of the same 'machine'. Once it is finished, each group can show the other group what they have done.

RATIONALE   *This exercise uses the idea of mechanical movements as an exploration in unspoken complicity. They are learning to express their individual creativity; to trust each other; and to accept the creative input of other people.*

Machines That Do Something

Staying in the two groups, each group has to decide on a machine for doing something. Then, with mechanical movements and sounds, they have to 'build' their machine together, using only their bodies and voices. When they have finished, each group can watch the other and try to guess what the machine is for.

RATIONALE   *As above, this exercise helps them to work together as a group, sharing ideas and creativity.*

Impossible Machines

Each group now has to decide on a machine that is impossible and fantastical. The examples I give them are 'a machine to create love between nations' and 'a machine to create a work of art'. They then have to discuss the necessary ingredients for their impossible machine and 'build' it together using only sounds and movements. The ingredients for creating a work of art could be, for instance, 'inspiration,' 'technique,' 'colour,' 'something to say,' 'beauty,' etc. It has to be as mechanical as the other machines, and it also has to have repetitious movements and sounds. Each person must know what ingredient they are representing.

RATIONALE   *The final exercise in this series helps the improvisers get used to the concept of 'thinking outside the box'. They listen to the ground rules. They obey them. And then they are shown how far they can step beyond the mundane.*

DEBRIEFING   *At this point it is worth discussing the 'machine' exercises and finding out what worked and what didn't. You can then talk about the impossible machines and point out that they could have created impossible machines when they were originally asked to 'create machines that do something'. They were obeying the ground rules when they made their 'sausage machines,' or their 'bubble-gum machines,' but they were limiting their creativity by not making impossible machines. Let's face it, any machine made with the human bodies is impossible, so why didn't they allow the 'product' of that machine to be impossible too. They weren't told that they couldn't. They put their own limitations on themselves. This is where they can start to realise that as long as they obey the established rules and listen carefully to the instructions they can let their imagination fly in any fantastical, creative manner that they like.*

Arguments

Divide the group up into pairs and, with all pairs working at the same time, ask each pair to improvise an argument. They are usually quite good at this, but if they seem to be a bit tentative, you can ask them to do it in stages, as follows:

Tell them that they are close friends and ask them to improvise a *disagreement* about something: a film, a TV star, favourite food, etc.

When that is established, don't let them stop the disagreement, but just tell them that they should start to get *irritated* with each other.

Next, tell them that they should get *cross*.

Finally, tell them that they should get really *angry* with each other.

RATIONALE   *This exercise, and the next one are to prepare them for the 'Adjusting the Scenario' improvisation.*

As I said earlier, I usually discourage arguments in improvisation, because they are often an excuse to be aggressive, and usually end up in a stalemate shouting match, but as preparation for the next two exercises, an argument gives them 'permission' to get into a confrontational mood.

Complaining About Loud Music

Divide the group into new sets of pairs. Then, with all the pairs improvising at the same time but separate from each other, tell them that the people in each pair are two people living in separate flats. One person lives in the flat below the other person's flat, and the one upstairs is playing loud music. Ask them to decide which is which. The improvisation starts when the person from downstairs goes to complain about the music. Let the improvisation continue for about four minutes and see what happens. After the previous exercise, most of them will be quite confrontational and uncompromisingly self-righteous.

RATIONALE   *This is the set-up for 'Adjusting the Scenario'.*

DEBRIEFING   *In a group discussion, point out that most of them adopted a very conventional approach to this scenario. They were good at being confrontational, but is that the only thing that could have happened?*

⚡ Improvisations

⚡ Adjusting the Scenario

After they have done the preparation exercises, ask the improvisers to divide themselves up into new sets of pairs so that everyone will be working with a different person. Then the whole group watches each new pair perform the same improvisation as before, only this time the improvisers are each given a secret objective.

The improvisation scenario is: a person in a flat below who asks the person in a flat above to turn the music down.

Before each pair starts, they have to decide who is going to be in the flat upstairs and who is going to be in the flat downstairs, and then they are each given one of the following 'adjustment to the scenario' secret objectives:

• Upstairs — *you're happily getting ready for your new boyfriend / girlfriend to arrive.*
  Downstairs — *you're studying for an important exam tomorrow.*

- Upstairs — *you've just split up from a relationship and you are drowning your sorrows in sombre classical music.*
  Downstairs — *you're waiting for your new boyfriend / girlfriend to arrive and sombre music will spoil the romantic atmosphere.*

- Upstairs — *you're listening to a new recording by your favourite band.*
  Downstairs — *the music upstairs is the band you hate the most.*

- Upstairs — *you're excitedly getting ready for a blind date to arrive.*
  Downstairs — *you are a new tenant and when the person upstairs opens the door you realise it is the person you saw on the stairs yesterday that you really fancy.*

- Upstairs — *the music is the new demo tape of the band you sing with.*
  Downstairs — *you are a guitarist and the music you hear coming from upstairs has a terrible guitarist on it.*

- Upstairs — *you are sorting out the right music for a party that you are having this evening.*
  Downstairs — *you have a hangover from a party you went to last night.*

- Upstairs — *you are practising your dancing because you are going clubbing tonight.*
  Downstairs — *you used to go out with the lead singer of the band you can hear being played upstairs and now you hate him / her.*

- Upstairs — *you are really lonely.*
  Downstairs — *you are just looking for an excuse to chat.*

- Upstairs — *you are a bit drunk.*
  Downstairs — *you love any excuse to gossip.*

- Upstairs — *you're just about to go down to check if the music is too loud.*
  Downstairs — *after you knock on the door you change your mind about complaining.*

RATIONALE   *All these improvisations are faithful to the scenario, but by giving a variety of alternative additions or adjustments it gives them a practical application of how to adjust a scenario.*

Session Debriefing

The discussion should centre on the endless possibilities that are available when two people are given a scenario to improvise. People should listen to the ground rules and then see how they can embellish them in their own way.

This is a strange session in some ways because it is trying to teach people how to lose their inhibitions and trust their imagination and creativity. It is teaching them to be bold within the limits of the 'given circumstances,' and as such is part of the ongoing exploration of creativity and originality that all people in the arts are continually engaged in.

But it is also important for another reason. This is the second occasion that each person has the experience of being observed by the rest of the group while they are improvising and if people are still 'playing to the audience' or 'trying to be funny,' then that can be pointed out to them. Some people will be physically facing 'the audience' while they talk to someone standing next to them, rather like a pair of stand-up comedians. Some will be trying to get into good positions 'on the stage'. They must really understand that those things are not important.

Sometimes the people who are watching say they can't hear the improvisation because the improvisers are talking too quietly, but this is also wrong thinking because these improvisations are not meant to be for the audience. I always say, 'If you can't hear, then get closer.' In fact, being able to hear people improvising is not important at all, since these improvisations are for the improvisers to explore and discover for themselves; they are not to entertain the viewers.

6

Emotions

We are all so interested in each other's emotions that we continually say things like: 'How are you feeling?', 'You alright?', 'What's up?' and, of course, 'How do you do?' We're also obsessed with letting the rest of the world know about our emotions as in 'I'm so stressed' or 'I'm so-o-o-o-o happy' or 'It makes me mad!' or 'I'm bored.' We talk about emotions all the time. We are born emotional. The first thing a baby does is cry. And then we get so excited about the baby's first smile because we know that all human beings are looking for happiness. Sit in a pub where people are watching a game of football and you get a demonstration of the whole gamut of emotions from euphoria to tears. And that's why they are there! Of course they want their team to win so they can be HAPPY, but they know that if their team doesn't win at least they can allow themselves to be communally DISTRAUGHT and let their ANGER out on the referee or the other team. And finally, when all is said and done, they can express their LOVE for each other as they share all the other emotions.

When I was in my late teens I enrolled for a stage management course at RADA, and my eyes were opened to the world of emotions in a way that I had never experienced before. Of course I had experienced the ups and downs of childhood and the various emotions that were thrown up by the need to understand the world and to survive, but actually, my childhood was a pretty easy-going affair. In fact, I was taught not to be too emotional. Keep a stiff upper lip. Don't wash your dirty linen in public. My family frowned on any excessively flamboyant display of emotion. It wasn't the right way to behave.

Yes, of course I was sometimes happy, sometimes sad, sometimes bored, sometimes in love, sometimes cross, sometimes even angry. But it wasn't until I was a student at RADA that I realised I had intense emotions. It wasn't until that time that I experienced BLIND RAGE.

I came from a small suburban town and rarely mixed with people from other backgrounds so it was a bit of a surprise to arrive in Gower Street and find myself mixing with a group of teenagers from other places and other cultures. We had an American girl in our group who looked like a glamour model, was from New York and said she knew Bob Dylan. There was a boy I got very friendly with who came from Oswaldtwistle in Lancashire – his father was a miner and he spoke with a strong Northern accent. There was a lesbian. I'd never met a lesbian. At least I didn't think I had. In fact, now I come to think of it, I didn't even know lesbians existed. We became good friends. There was also a guy who played the trumpet and had recently been

busking in the south of France. He never washed his socks, he said, he just wore them till they were disgusting, then threw them away and bought a new pair. He also said, 'I grow my hair long because my ears stick out.' Strange, I thought: if you're trying to disguise a flawed personal feature, you rather lose the point if you tell everyone about it. He also said he was sure that we'd meet again after we had finished the course. That was forty years ago and I'm still waiting.

Then there was Christopher.

Christopher was a public-school boy and was very confident, if not to say arrogant. He didn't smile much, seemed to know lots of rich, famous people. His father was a well-known actor and his sister's best friend went out with one of The Beatles. I don't really remember the details, but I was very impressed, and he made me feel extremely suburban and middle class. And he made me feel that both of those things were the worst things you could possibly be. I couldn't escape my background. Luckily I was excellent at stage management so at least that gave me some status.

The stage management course was new and, because they hadn't provided enough lockers for us all to have one of our own, we had to share them. I shared mine with Christopher. I didn't choose this, nor did he. We were just given a key each.

No problem really because the lockers were big enough and neither of us had much stuff. One day I put a bottle of beer in our locker in case I really needed a relaxing drink at some future date. A few days later, after a particularly exhausting day, I went to get my bottle of beer and it was gone. I couldn't believe it. I knew I couldn't have made a mistake. I knew Christopher must have taken it. I was gobsmacked. Nothing in my upbringing had prepared me for this utter betrayal of trust. I went to the common room and found Christopher telling everyone about some famous person he had been at school with. I was pretty cross, but I held myself together.

'Have you taken my bottle of beer?'

'What bottle of beer?'

'The one in our locker!!'

'Oh, was that yours?'

'!*!*!*!'

Was that mine? Of course it was mine. Who else's could it have been? We were the only people with keys to the locker. Was it mine? Was it mine, you arrogant little toad? Was it mine?

I didn't say any of that. I was entering a Blind Rage for the first time in my life and I was speechless. My blood was boiling. I turned on my heel and walked off into the night. It was December and it was raining.

I walked and walked, turning this way left and that way right. I was in such a rage that I didn't notice the rain and I didn't know what I was doing or where I was going. After about an hour I must have calmed down a bit because I realised that I was totally lost. I realised that I didn't have a coat. And I realised that I was wet through! I can honestly say that I hadn't noticed any of this all the time I was walking, all I knew was that I was experiencing a *very strong emotion* for the *first time in my life*.

I don't remember what happened next, but I bet I never spoke to Christopher much again. He became an actor too but we never met. He has no idea what effect he had on my life. He has no idea that he introduced me to Blind Rage and even if he did, he probably couldn't care less.

'What bottle of beer?'

'Oh, was that yours?'

Fie, fie, fie!

The other contact I had with emotion that year was when I was stage managing a play for the drama students at RADA. There was a Japanese girl in one of the plays – by George Bernard Shaw, I think. She was playing a chirpy maid. One evening she was just totally sobbing in the wings waiting to go on. I asked one of the other actors what the matter was and they told me her boyfriend had just dumped her and she was totally distraught.

I was very worried. I was in charge of the show and the 'chirpy maid' was sobbing in the wings. What could I do? My heart was beating and the seconds were ticking away. I tried to ask her how she was, but there was no getting through to her. Her cue was coming up. She was sobbing. I was panicking. Tick tock tick tock – and here comes her cue. She flicked the tears from her face with a handkerchief, put on a smile, stepped onto the stage, chirped merrily through her maid's lines, turned back to the wings, made her exit and burst into tears again.

She did that all evening. Each time she went on stage she was as bright as a button and each time she came off into the wings she was a sobbing mess.

I learned something about actors that evening. I learned how dedicated they are to the job and I learned how they are able to control their emotions. In fact, actors become skilled practitioners of emotion. It's one of the tools of their trade.

The Lifeblood of Drama

HUMAN BEINGS ARE IN A CONSTANT STATE OF EMOTIONAL flux and we all have a massive range of subtly different emotions that ebb and flow continuously. When actors are working on a text, they are always searching for the *emotional journey* of their character. They constantly ask themselves how their character 'feels' so that they can enter a new scene bringing a backlog of emotional influences.

The funny thing is, when inexperienced people start an improvisation they usually don't bring any particular emotions into the scene with them, and although it is fair to say that in real life our emotional state can often be rather nondescript or undefined, it's never non-existent. And how much more interesting life is when you are in a highly charged emotional state. Even discussing the weather can be exciting when you are in love, and playing a game of cards can be quite dynamic when you are repressing your anger.

Emotion brings passion, humour, suspense, dynamics and tension to an improvisation. It is the lifeblood of drama.

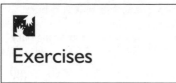

Exercises

Poppy/Power

Ask everyone to shut their eyes and walk carefully around the room, letting their bodies gently brush past each other as they weave in and out. Ask them to whisper the word 'poppy' regularly as they go. This allows them to experience vulnerability and anxiety.

After they have practised that, ask them to open their eyes and stride forcibly around the room saying the word 'power' quietly but aggressively to themselves and to each other, so they can experience authority and confidence.

Then ask half the group to be 'power' and half to be 'poppies' and let them walk around intermingling. The 'poppies' have to keep their eyes shut, but the 'power' people can have theirs open. After a while get them to reverse roles and carry on for a bit longer.

Now that they have practised these two emotional states, select one person from the group and while the rest of the group shuts their eyes as before and walks carefully around the room saying the word 'poppy', the other person walks confidently amongst them with his or her eyes open, forcibly saying the word 'power'. The solo person then picks on one of the 'poppies', holds them by the shoulder and says 'power' firmly, aggressively, but quietly into their ear. That person then joins the first and they both walk confidently around the room saying 'power' while the others continue to keep their eyes shut and say 'poppy'. The two 'power' people each pick another 'poppy' to dominate who then joins them to make four, etc. etc., until everyone is a 'power' person searching for a 'poppy' to intimidate.

RATIONALE   *This exercise (which is an adaptation of an exercise described by Augusto Boal in* Games for Actors and Non-actors) *is about oppression and the exploitation of power. But used in this context it becomes an introduction to two extremes of emotion.*

◼ Emotional Objects

Ask the group to stand in a circle. Then ask one to hold an imaginary *Christmas tree decoration* in their hand. Tell them that it is beautiful and delicate and that they love it. Ask the group to pass it carefully round the circle, and see if they can each make it real for themselves, at the same time feeling the sense of wonder and beauty that Christmas brings.

When they have all had a go, ask them to pass an imaginary handful of disgusting *slime* round the circle and explore how they feel about that.

Then ask them to pass an imaginary photograph around, but as each person receives it, they must imagine it is a photograph of a *person that they really love*.

Then they can pass an imaginary *kitten*.

Then they can pass an imaginary *skull*.

(If you select your own objects to pass round the circle, they should be objects that generate particular emotions.)

I always end with an imaginary *ticking bomb* which is about to go off. After they have all passed it round, I make a 'bang' noise without them seeing (I usually hit a table or a chair and say: 'Bang!'), and they all jump.

RATIONALE   *By having imaginary objects to spark their imaginations, they are able to use the 'memory' of the object to stimulate their 'memory' of the emotion.*

⚡ Improvisations

⚡ Improvisation Cards

This will probably be the first time that you are using the Improvisation Cards, so you need to show them to the group and explain how they work.

At this stage you should only use the Simple Scenario Cards. The other Scenario Cards should be used later in the training when the group are more confident in improvising truthfully, and the Character Cards would only add complications at this point. (The use of Character Cards is described in detail in Chapter 9: Character.)

To use the cards, they should be fanned out and held face down so the improvisers can only see the back of the cards – rather like a magician when he asks someone to 'pick a card'.

Divide the group up into pairs and ask one person from each pair to come and pick a Simple Scenario Card. Ask them to give each other roles if that is required (e.g. in the 'teacher and a student' scenario, one role is the 'teacher' and the other role is the 'student'.)

When they have done that, all the pairs should improvise their scenes at the same time, keeping them simple and realistic and just bringing their natural emotions to the scene.

RATIONALE   *This is purely an introduction to the Scenario Cards.*

DEBRIEFING   *Discuss how they felt about the scene. Was it realistic? Was it easy? Was it difficult? If they felt it was difficult, remind them that they don't have to 'do' anything, they just have to 'be there' and behave naturally. You can also clear up any questions about the cards.*

⚡ Emotional Improvisations

Ask them to perform the scenes again, but this time each pair improvises in front of the rest of the group. Before a pair start, each improviser should secretly be given an emotion chosen from the following list:

Angry	Frightened
Amazed	Guilty
Annoyed	Happy
Anxious	Hopeful
Ashamed	In love
Confused	Irritated
Content	Jealous
Curious	Panicky
Dreamy	Remorseful
Disgusted	Sad
Embarrassed	Self-righteous

They should be given a short time to think about the emotion and to decide what could have caused it, and then they should improvise the scene again.

The important thing to tell them is that they should *bring the emotional state into the scene with them*. The emotion should not be directed at the other improviser, nor should it be caused by the scene. It should be caused by something that has happened *before* the scene. In a lot of cases they should be trying to overcome this emotional state in order to progress with the scene. For instance, if their role is a shop assistant and their emotional state is 'Angry' then they will have to try to control that emotion otherwise the customer would walk out without buying anything. *It doesn't mean they are angry with the customer.*

Similarly, if their emotional state is 'In Love', that doesn't mean they will immediately fall in love with the customer or that they will only talk about romantic things. They are selling shoes. That is what the scene is about. The emotion is the subtext. They should keep it 'sub', and not make it the 'text'.

Session Debriefing

Discuss with the group how the addition of emotions has affected their scenes. Adding emotions will probably have made improvising easier for them because they are using their acting skills and because they have to focus and concentrate within the scene. Also, there will have been some exciting or amusing changes to the scene because of the emotions. By this stage, any humour in the scene will start to come out of the truth of the situation rather than by the use of gags and funny lines.

Explain to them that they should always bring some sort of emotion to a scene, however subtle it might be. It doesn't have to be an emotion that would appear to be appropriate to the scene.

Important Note

If at this stage the improvisers are still trying to be funny, they should be reminded yet again about the purpose of this kind of improvisation. It's not to amuse an audience!! As the improvising sessions progress they should feel less and less that they need to entertain the spectators because they will be given more and more techniques to enable them to keep their concentration within the reality of the scene.

7

Activities

Remarkable things, human beings: they can walk and talk at the same time. Is that what they call multitasking: talking about something but at the same time doing something entirely different? While I was training for the London Marathon, jogging along at my maximum speed of about five-and-a-half miles per hour, I'd often hear a couple of people behind me chatting about their day at work or the problems with their love life. At first I would think they were on bicycles because their voices seemed to get louder as they came up behind me. But no, they were running too. Really running. Going faster than me and then flying by. These people were properly training. They were conscious of their running style, they were breathing correctly and they were mentally monitoring their pace so they could cover whatever distance they had set out for themselves. And yet at the same time they could talk about some incident at work that had been hard to handle or they could share the emotional ups and downs of their love lives with each other.

In the past I have done a lot of painting and decorating, and I'd often get someone to do it with me in order to get the job done more quickly. Or so I said. But what I really wanted was company. I wanted to have someone to talk to. The funny thing was that the conversations I had with fellow painters and decorators were always fantastic.

You could really indulge in the details of a story as you rolled paint onto the walls; you could get into deep emotional matters as you undercoated the window frames; pasting wallpaper inspired philosophical analysis of popular music; hanging it, and holidays were discussed; films; novels; relationships; life in general – at the same time you never stopped decorating. In fact, the very act of applying paint to a wall or a door frame somehow freed the mind to roam into any area of conversation that you wanted. Trivial, meaningful, romantic, funny . . . you name it.

It often amuses me that actors on television just stand and stare at each other while they play a scene, when in real life we are often doing things and speaking to each other at the same time. A long time ago there was a TV series about fighter pilots in the First World War. Two young actors played the flying heroes. I vividly remember watching a scene where the two actors were putting on their flying gear before they went off in their World War One open-cockpit aeroplanes. Open-cockpit! They must have been freezing. The two actors had very different ways of putting on their flying jackets and scarves, etc. The first one put the scarf loosely round his neck so he looked good and then slipped his arms into the sleeves of his jacket, pulled it on and stood there with it unbuttoned

so he could carry on talking and still be seen by the camera. Pretty standard stuff, and I wouldn't have thought too much about it unless the other actor hadn't approached the scene with a real focus on what his character was actually about to do. He continued to talk but at the same time you could tell that he was putting on warm clothes in order to go flying in the freezing cold, open-cockpit aeroplane.

Funnily enough, I happened to know that the second actor was a motorcyclist and he knew what it meant to put on the proper clothing to keep warm. While the two actors spoke the dialogue, this second actor carefully wrapped his flying scarf around his neck, making sure that there was no gap where the cold air could get in, then he put on his flying jacket and carefully buttoned up each of the buttons, checking that they were done properly. He made sure the scarf was tucked into the collar of the jacket and he made sure that the bottom of the jacket was pulled snugly over the tops of his trousers. Then, still playing the scene, still talking, he sat down to put on his flying boots, taking the same sort of care and was just getting his leather flying hat ready when the scene ended. As they left the room, you really felt that the second actor was going to fly an aeroplane, whereas the first actor looked like he was just leaving the set at the end of a scene.

It was fascinating. Several scenes later, after they had flown their mission, they came back into the same room with very dirty faces. The make-up department had painted on the grime so it looked as if they had been wearing goggles. The first actor wiped the make-up off his face with a towel while they acted the scene, but the second actor, the actor who had been very careful with his dressing procedures, spoke all his lines with his face over a basin making sure that he was thoroughly washing all the grime from the corner of his eyes and from the edge of his nose, etc. While they talked you couldn't see his face at all, you could only see his back hunched over the basin as he washed.

It struck me as very truthful. This attention to physical action made me believe that the second actor really had been flying. But not only that: I noticed that somehow the dialogue seemed to come alive. His words took on the rhythms of natural speech as he broke up sentences to wash round his mouth and slightly stumbled to think of a word as he multi-tasked. Also, of course, from his awkward position over the basin he really had to try to communicate his thoughts to the other actor. It's that need to communicate that makes acting come alive.

Mimed Activities

IF YOU ASK INEXPERIENCED PEOPLE TO IMPROVISE A SCENE they will often sit down side by side and just talk. Or they will face each other and stare intently into each other's eyes to have their conversation. So in order to start incorporating an activity into an improvisation, people need to practise doing something while they talk. It's not that difficult. In real life they do it all the time. People talk while they are driving a car; they talk while they are clearing up the kitchen or chopping vegetables; they even talk while they are playing *Grand Theft Auto*!

The trouble with improvising a scene and doing an activity is that the improvisers are not in a real car. They are not in a real kitchen. They don't have the game console in their hands. They have to imagine these things. If they are chopping vegetables, they have to mime the knife, the chopping board, the carrots, and sometimes even the table they are sitting at. It's not easy. Especially when they are making up the words as they go along.

85

But as soon as they get used to adding physical activities to an improvisation, their concentration increases, the scene begins to feel more realistic, and the dialogue starts to come alive.

Exercises

Magic Modelling Clay

Ask the group to stand in a circle and tell them you have a piece of invisible magic modelling clay. Tell them that they can mould it into anything they like, but it must be something they can physically use or do something with. It can get larger and it can get smaller, all they have to do is mime moulding it into an object. I usually demonstrate this by moulding the imaginary clay into an imaginary tennis racket and then using the imaginary tennis racket to serve an imaginary tennis ball, and they have to guess what it is.

The game is that having used my imaginary object, I pass it to the next person round the circle who first of all has to mime using my object and then has to mime moulding the magic modelling clay into anything that they want it to be. When they have done that, they have to mime using their new imaginary object in an appropriate way until the person next to them guesses what it is. It's usually quite easy, but if not, you can ask everyone in the group to shout out what they think it is until someone gets it right. After the object has been identified, the second person passes it on to the third person, who uses it, then moulds the clay into something else and uses that, and so on, round the circle until everyone has had a go.

RATIONALE *This exercise helps them to imagine the details of an object and 'feel' it in their hands. If they can get used to miming things accurately, it can help them believe that imaginary objects are actually there.*

🔥 Playing and Chatting

I usually make this exercise carry on from the previous exercise, so they can use the object they have 'created'. But it's important that the object is something they can play with. Something they can imagine holding in their hands and imagine moving about. A tennis ball. A hula-hoop. A skipping rope. Anything that keeps them physically occupied. Something they can really get the feel of. (If they have created an object that they can't do much with, ask them to make a new object and then start using that.)

With everyone working on their own in different parts of the room, ask them to use their object and get to know it. How heavy is it? How does it move? What happens to it when they drop it to the ground? Ask them to examine it and play with it until they start to feel that it really exists and they are absolutely comfortable with their mime.

Then ask them to start having conversations with other people in the room. Tell them they must continue to mime playing with their imaginary objects while they talk, and they mustn't talk about the object they are playing with. They should talk about other subjects: like going clubbing this evening or their favourite food. They could talk about pets or the town they come from, but they must continue to play with their object as they chat. And both chatting and playing should each be as important as the other, but separate. Their physical attention should be on the object and their mental attention should be on the conversation.

RATIONALE   *This exercise enables them to get used to 'doing something' while they improvise dialogue. They have become very familiar with their objects and they are having very simple conversations, so this difficult technique is made as straightforward as possible.*

DEBRIEFING   *Because it's hard to do, they should be allowed to discuss the difficulties of this exercise. But it is also important for them to under-stand how their vocal rhythms and inflections changed and how the dialogue became more 'real' when they were doing something.*

Improvisations

Simple Flat-Share Activities

Ask everyone to get into pairs and set up an improvisation where they are two people sharing a flat. They should decide what their relationship is: best friends, brothers and sisters, or whatever. Then they must decide how the flat is arranged. Where is the kitchen? Where are the bedrooms? Where is the furniture? This only needs to take a couple of minutes.

Then, with all the pairs working together in different parts of the room, let them improvise as flat-sharers for about four minutes.

When they have done this, ask them each to think of some sort of activity they could be doing in the flat: cutting their nails, building a house of cards, sewing on a button, etc. Something small and contained but physically active. Something they can really focus their attention on as they talk. Then, with each person working on their own for a couple of minutes, ask them to concentrate on perfecting the mime of their activity. (Make sure they haven't decided to read a book or watch television because those are mental activities rather than physical activities. As are writing letters or playing computer games.)

When they have done that, ask each pair to repeat their flat-share improvisation, but this time, they should be doing the activity they have just practised while having more or less the same conversation they had before.

RATIONALE   *These activities make the improvisations come alive as the improvisers become more focused and involved in the scene.*

DEBRIEFING   *Discuss the differences that these activities bring to an improvisation and how hard they were to do.*

⚡ Complicated Flat-Share Activities

Ask everyone to get into different pairs and, as before, decide their relationship and plan the layout of their flat. Then ask each pair to choose a more adventurous activity, like cooking a meal together, or cleaning the flat, or moving the furniture around. They should choose an activity that needs a certain amount of verbal communication in order to do it, but one that can be done while they have a conversation about something else. So that, for instance, part of the time they could be talking about something that happened last night and part of the time they could be asking each other to 'Pass the cooking oil', or they could talk about going shopping together, and also say things like: 'Let's put the sofa over there.'

With all the pairs working at the same time, they should be given the chance to practise this improvisation. Then, one pair at a time, they can show their improvisations to the rest of the group.

RATIONALE   *Although these improvisations will have been quite difficult to do, when people watch each other improvise, they will see how truthful the scenes have become. The dialogue will have taken on the more natural rhythm of everyday speech: there will have been hesitations; there will have been sudden rushes of words; there will have been pauses; etc. etc. Not only that but, because they will have been distracted by their activities, their voices will have used the inflections and emphases that human beings need to be able to communicate clearly and positively with each other.*

Session Debriefing

Discuss the whole session and how activities can be used in future improvisations. It will be difficult to find suitable activities for some of the scenarios they will be asked to improvise. For instance, if they are shopping, they may wonder what else they could be doing. But there are lots of things. They could concentrate on tiny personal activities, like having an annoying broken nail, or playing with their keys, or coping with a pair of trousers that are on the brink of falling down. Or they could use more subtle activities, like keeping an eye on the street outside because their best friend who is in another shop doesn't know they went into this particular shop. If they think about it, there are lots of things they could be doing. They don't have to be interesting activities. They just have to try to keep themselves physically occupied.

There is no doubt that it is harder to mime an activity than it is to use real objects, so the concentration involved in improvising and miming at the same time is quite intense. However, the very nature of that intense concentration causes the improvisers to focus more deeply on the improvisation. And as I have said before, the more they concentrate and the more they have to think about during an improvisation, the less likely they are to feel that they need to entertain whoever is watching. The improvisation itself becomes the purpose of the improvisation.

8

Objectives

'What are you trying to prove?' That's what people say, isn't it? And they say things like 'What are you doing that for?' or 'What do you want me to say?' or 'What are you trying to achieve?'

Or sometimes they shout in frustration – 'What do you want?'

These are everyday questions in real life but they are also questions that actors continually ask of the characters they are trying to understand. 'What does my character want? What is my character's *objective*?'

A couple of years ago I took up running because a friend of mine had just completed the London Marathon and she was so elated that it made me want some of the same sort of elation in my own life. I had never run before, and the next London Marathon would take place on about the same date as a particularly large round-numbered birthday of mine, so I started training. It was very hard to start with, but I set myself the task because I wanted to celebrate this particular birthday with an achievement. I had an objective.

To cut to the chase, I achieved my objective and completed the course in five hours 25 minutes. I came something like 29,875th, but I did it! And I lost a stone during the training. In fact, I was so pleased about losing weight that I carried on running four times a week after the marathon just to keep my weight down. After a couple of months it was three or four times a week. Then it became two or three. Eventually once a week, and then finally I haven't run for about a month. I keep saying I will start up again when the weather gets better. (But will I?)

And here's the reason that it's hard to run this year – I don't have *an objective* any more. I applied to run in the London Marathon for a second time but I didn't get a place. I'm not really overweight and I'm not particularly unfit, so there was nothing to get me out there, pounding the streets. No objectives. Objectives are driving forces. They make us do things.

No wonder Stanislavsky had a field day on this subject.

And it's not as simplistic and straightforward as it might appear. There are super-objectives: what does your character want out of life; there are everyday objectives: what does your character want today and why is he or she having the conversation anyway. And there are objectives governing each line your character says (sometimes called 'actions'). There are even objectives governing your character's choice of words, and, in the case of Shakespeare, there are objectives governing why your character sometimes speaks in verse and sometimes speaks in prose; why your character uses rhetoric and why he or she doesn't.

It's a very complex issue.

What Does My Character Want?

A CHARACTER'S OBJECTIVES ARE OF MAJOR SIGNIFICANCE for actors. They are always searching for clues as to why their character says or does what they say or do. They want to know why. Why? Why does my character say this? What is the reason my character does that? What is my character's objective? What's the OBJECTIVE??!!

The funny thing is that in improvisation, people rarely think of objectives when they go into a scene, and if they do, the objectives are usually rather prosaic.

The improvisation is someone buying a pair of shoes.

'What is your objective?'

'I want to buy a pair of shoes.'

Yes, well . . . How interesting is that?

So before someone starts to improvise a scene, they should always ask themselves: 'Apart from the obvious, what else could my character want?' With the above scene it could be a number of things. For instance, the objective could be to spend less than £30 on shoes, or it could be to buy a pair of black shoes with gold buckles. Even these simple objectives give an improviser more to work with than just: 'I want to buy a pair of shoes.'

On the other hand, the objective could be more extreme. It could be that they've come to buy a pair of shoes because they want to ask the shop assistant out on a date, or that their objective is to get a twenty per cent discount on any shoes they buy.

Then there are hidden objectives. The kind that probably won't be revealed during the improvisation. They could be buying a pair of shoes to impress a boyfriend/girlfriend; or to look good for an upcoming interview; or to replace a pair that got lost on holiday.

Whether they are part of the action, or buried deep in the subtext, objectives affect the way people behave and continually drive their actions. Improvisers can use that driving force to help them be more creative.

Exercises

Supermarket

Set up some chairs in the room so they represent three or four aisles in a supermarket and ask the whole group to go shopping. At this stage each person should be shopping on their own, although the rest of the group will all be in the supermarket, shopping at the same time. Each person must know whether they are pushing a trolley or carrying a basket. They must know what they want to buy and whether or not they know where to find it. They must know what is on the shelves, and they must also know what they can or cannot afford. They must know what they are taking off the shelves and what they are putting in their trolley or basket. They must know how much the basket weighs or how easy it is to push the trolley. (I usually let them start 'shopping', and then talk them through these things during the exercise.) As they shop they can have conversations with other shoppers if they need to, but only as much as they would if they were shopping for real. Everyone in the improvisation should be a shopper, no one should work for the supermarket, and no one should finish their shopping and go to the check-out.

When the group have been shopping for a few minutes, ask them to choose one of the other people in the group and think of a reason they want to avoid that person. Maybe it is an ex-boyfriend. Maybe it is someone they owe money to, but, whatever it is, they must try never to be in the same aisle as that person.

Of course, they have to continue shopping.

When that is established, tell them that they spot someone up the other end of the aisle that they fancy and that they want to try to get close to that person. (I usually tell them that gender is not an issue in this exercise. Of course they can fancy someone from the opposite sex if they want to, but boys can also fancy boys and girls can fancy girls.) They still have to avoid the first person that they picked out, but now they have to try to get close to the second person at the same time.

And they can talk.

And they have to keep on shopping.

As time ticks by they have to think of a way they could initiate a conversation with the person they fancy.

And they still have to avoid the first person.

And they still have to keep shopping.

Once they have established contact with the person they fancy, they then have to see if they can get a date. They still have to shop and they still have to try to avoid the first person, but they have to try to get a date.

This can become mayhem, but it's worth letting it continue for a while to see if anyone achieves their objective.

(As I said, you can talk them through this exercise as they do it. Once they start shopping they have to continue to stay in the improvisation, but you can shout out the new instructions as they come up.)

RATIONALE   *This exercise establishes a scenario – shopping – and then introduces two objectives, one at a time – avoidance and then connection. The objectives should be the subtext of a scene. The 'sur-text', as it were, is the shopping. Improvisers will often want to abandon the sur-text, and let the subtext become the scenario. This exercise is to help them understand how to get the balance right. They may want to avoid someone and they may want to make a connection with someone else, but, above all, they have to keep shopping!*

DEBRIEFING   *After you stop them you can ask the improvisers to discuss whether anyone managed to get a date with another person, or what happened during the improvisation. They should understand that although this was just a fun exercise, the important thing is that they had objectives, and that the objectives should not have overwhelmed the scenario.*

Improvisations

Sea Cruise

Using the chairs again, it is possible to set up the room to be the deck of a cruise ship. I usually use the chairs to delineate an inside area with tables and chairs at one end of the room and an outside area which is the deck at the other end. I usually let the deck also run along the sides of the room. This deck area would also have some chairs on it.

Before they start, tell them that they are all passengers on a cruise ship; it is the first day out at sea and no one knows anyone else – apart from one couple. Choose the two who are going to be that one couple and then give each person in the group a secret objective using the list below (the top two objectives are for each of the two people who are a couple):

Couple

> To make your partner jealous   To brag that you have an attractive partner

Each of the others

> To find a wealthy investor   To find a new lover
>
> To be popular   To con money from people
>
> To find someone to blackmail   To convert people to your spiritual beliefs
>
> To gather and spread gossip   To spread lies about yourself
>
> To pick arguments   To talk about ecological matters
>
> To get drunk and have fun   To win money at cards
>
> To write poetry   To cure your depression
>
> To learn English better   To let people know you were once in a reality TV show
>
> To keep fit and get a tan   To get everyone involved in a show at the end of the week

This improvisation can go on for quite a long time – fifteen or twenty minutes – to give people a chance to mingle and move about.

As always, they should use their own names.

RATIONALE   *This group improvisation is to give them the opportunity to see if they can keep focused on their objectives while they are talking to people who are also focused on their own objectives. It's all very well to try to achieve an objective, but if someone else has an entirely different objective to achieve, it can be quite hard to stay focused.*

DEBRIEFING   *Find out what happened. Who achieved their objectives and who didn't. It is fun to get each person to tell everyone what their objective was and to see if other people had guessed it or not.*

⚡ Conflicting Objectives

The group should be divided up into pairs to suit the gender combinations available for the set of improvisations listed below. Each pair should improvise in front of the rest of the group, so that people can learn from watching each other.

The following is a set of improvisations for two people. Each person is given a secret objective which the other doesn't know about. It must be impressed on them that these improvisations are more serious than the 'Supermarket' exercise, and they should make them as realistic as possible. They should definitely not let the objective overwhelm the improvisation, but they should aim to achieve their objective in a realistic way. These improvisations are gender specific, apart from one which is also for three people in case there are an odd number in the group.

Tell each pair the scenario of their improvisation and then whisper secretly to each person their specific objectives as listed below:

ONE MALE AND ONE FEMALE

* Flat-sharing partners on a bus going to the movies.

  Male: *To persuade your partner that the two of you should get a pet.*

  Female: *To persuade your partner that the two of you should move into a less dangerous part of town.*

* Long-term boyfriend and girlfriend sitting in church after a service.

  Female: *To tell your boyfriend that you want to become a nun.*

  Male: *To ask your girlfriend to marry you.*

* Father and daughter meeting in a fancy restaurant after she has been backpacking around the world for a year.

  Male: *To tell your daughter that you have let her room and she can't come back home to live.*

  Female: *To tell your dad that you're pregnant. You're not sure who the father is and you want to come home to have the baby.*

- Married couple with no children having dinner at home together.

  Female: *To persuade your husband that the two of you can now buy an expensive sports car.*

  Male: *To persuade your wife that you can now afford to start a family.*

- Lovers having a last evening together because he is in the army and is going back to the Middle East tomorrow.

  Male: *To break off the relationship because the danger you face is too stressful for her.*

  Female: *To persuade your lover to run away from the army and not to go back to the war zone tomorrow.*

TWO FEMALES

- Two sisters in a taxi going shopping together. One is married to Dave, the other is engaged to Pete. Neither have children.

  Married sister: *To persuade your sister to get married to Pete.*

  Engaged sister: *To persuade your sister to leave Dave because you've found out that he has been seeing other women.*

- Two friends putting on make-up in the toilets of a club at midnight.

  One: *To persuade your friend that it's time to leave because you've had a bad time with a guy you've just met and think all men are bastards.*

  Two: *To persuade your friend to make up a foursome because you've just met these two guys in the club.*

TWO MALES

- Brothers at home watching TV and drinking beer. Mum and Dad have just gone away for the weekend.

  One: *To persuade your brother to leave home because he's such a slob and you want the bigger bedroom.*

  Two: *To persuade your brother to let you use his bedroom, which is quite small, as a chill-out room for a party you are having this evening.*

- Advertising agency boss and his employee in the pub after work.

  Boss: *To persuade your employee to hand in his notice and move on because his ideas are stale.*

  Employee: *To persuade your boss to give you a raise because more money would inspire you to work harder.*

THREE PEOPLE (ANY COMBINATION OF MALE AND FEMALE)

- Siblings meeting in the pub to talk about their elderly father's future. Mother died two years ago.

  One: *You have found out that your father has met another woman and you think he should get married again.*

  Two: *Your father seems to be spending a lot of money and you want to know where your inheritance is disappearing to.*

  Three: *You think your father is too old to look after himself and would be better off selling the house and moving into a nursing home.*

RATIONALE *The objectives in these improvisations are intentionally working in opposition to each other, and as each improviser becomes aware of the other's objective, the improvisation becomes more dynamic and fascinating. The improvisers will be learning to negotiate a scene and how to allow the drama to unfold.*

Session Debriefing

Discuss whether objectives help the improvisers and whether they make the improvisations more realistic. They should understand that in an improvisation where facts or 'plot' are gradually revealed, their characters should become aware of new information at exactly the same time that the improviser becomes aware. They shouldn't pretend they haven't realised (e.g. in the second improvisation: as soon at the male improviser suspects that the female improviser wants to become a nun, his suspicion should become a part of the improvisation. He shouldn't pretend he doesn't realise.)

Finally, it should be made clear to them, that they should take the time to give themselves an objective before they start any improvisations in the future.

9

Character

When I first put my photograph in *Spotlight* – the actor's directory – actors had to decide which category they wanted to go in. There were two categories for both men and women. In each case these were 'Leading' and 'Character'. It was a difficult choice for me because I didn't feel as if I was a leading man yet, but at the same time, everyone in the 'Character' category seemed to be really old. I plumped for 'Leading' and then went out into the wide world to play all those 'young men who are supposed to be in love with the young girl' parts, and you know what? I discovered that young people have character too! We all do! Everyone does!

I stayed in 'Leading' for a number of years, and by the time I was old enough to move into the 'Character' section, *Spotlight* had decided, quite rightly, that those categories were old-fashioned and didn't make much sense.

It was about this time in my life that I was asked to do some role-play work for a prominent bank. This wasn't your everyday high-street bank; it was a bank whose clients were often rich and powerful, so it was quite a sophisticated set-up. I joined a bunch of actors who had been gathered together to provide guinea-pig 'customers' so the bank employees could practise 'selling' the bank's financial products to us. These bank employees were also quite powerful. They were bank managers and area managers and young,

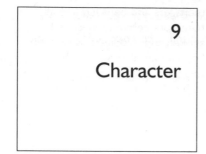

upwardly-mobile under-managers, who all thought they knew what they were doing, so were often quite resentful about the need for any training whatsoever.

Before we started work with the bank, each of the actors had to create a character in discussion with David, who was running these training days. Although we had to create characters who had lots of money, the process was quite complicated and the characters were quite varied. For instance, one of the actresses created the character of a girl in her mid-thirties who had been left a castle in Scotland, and one of the actors became an Australian businessman who was rather private about how he had made his money because it wasn't nec-essarily totally legal. For my role, David and I created the part of an airline executive in charge of maintenance with British Airways and who worked at Heathrow Airport. I had my own suit and with a bit of grooming I could easily look the part. As I said, I was the age for 'Character' parts by then.

Some of the aspects of my role were easy to come to terms with. I was supposed to be a family man, which I was. My imaginary role-play family could be exactly like my own family; after all, my real wife had quite an important job with the Royal Ballet and that was entirely suitable for an executive. We lived in Chiswick. That was okay. My children were

teenagers and behaved like all teenagers behave. I was well-spoken and middle-class, etc. etc. So that was all easy. But then there was the job I was supposed to have. An airline executive! I was told that people often don't go into much detail about their work because they think it will be boring for others, so as long as I read the paper to make sure there were no particular stories about Heathrow Airport in the news, I would be able to blag it. So far everything was fine. But the thing I had a big problem with was the fact that I was supposed to be earning £200,000 per annum! That's a lot of money. In those days I was lucky if I made £20,000. What would I have spent the other £180,000 on? What do people spend that sort of money on? Holidays? Diamonds? Gambling?

I was very nervous before the first session. Not only were these role-play interviews supposed to carry on for nearly an hour each, but the bank employees had been told that we were real people who had offered to help out. Would I be found out? Also I had to do this really subtle bit of acting because my character was going to be made redundant at the age of fifty and although he was going to be given a massive golden handshake (which was why he was talking to the bank in the first place), he was also feel-ing shattered, undermined and confused. But he was unable to let his insecurities show because of his pride! Talk about subtext!!

There I was, using all my confident, almost arrogant, executive body-language and modes of speech while underpinning my external behaviour was a deep sense of insecurity, doubt and failure. I have to say I was pretty subtle about it all.

The first session went well, and, although I was in quite a hyped-up state, I think they put my nervousness down to my impending redundancy. However, when they asked me whether I had invested any of my money I had to say I hadn't because that was something I (John Abbott) knew nothing about. In fact, I said I (my character) wasn't really interested in money and was useless when it came to thinking about it sensibly. That was easy to say, because that is what I'm like myself, so I could impose my own attitudes about money on my airline executive character. The person interviewing me seemed to accept that, so I felt that I more or less got away with it.

(Actually, after doing a few of these sessions I realised that the people interviewing me were far more nervous than I was, because they were being filmed, assessed and appraised by a small panel of instructors, and they were terrified of doing something wrong.)

Anyway, after I became used to these role-play sessions, I told David that I was worried that my character, who had a massive salary and was obviously loaded, had no interest in money and knew nothing about investments and such like. And here's the point. David, who had spent years devising and refining these role-play sessions, said, 'Don't worry about it. There are loads of people out there and they are all different. In my experience no one fits into a simple mould. You can create almost any sort of character, and be pretty certain that there will be someone like it out in the real world. People are always surprising and always interesting.'

Of course, being an actor I should have known that. I had been creating characters in plays and on television for years. But these were characters who had been invented by an author, and the actor's job was just a case of trying to recreate what the author had in mind. Actually, it made me feel rather unimaginative. As if I had always gone for the obvious. An executive earning £200,000 a year? He must be interested in money. I'll do some research into investments and suchlike. But according to David that would not necessarily be the case. Having learned that important lesson, I decided that from then on I would go for contrasts all the time in my acting roles. It seemed to be so much more interesting, and it threw up a really diverse range of character decisions. A doctor with no interest in humanity. A vicar who likes to put some money on the horses. A shy judge. A boxer who hates violence. You could go on for ever.

Taking on a New Character

So this exploration into character is also an intro-duction to the Character Cards that can be used in conjunction with the Scenario Cards.

First of all, I have to make clear the distinction between my use of the words 'role' and 'character' in this context. The 'role' that you might be asked to improvise is the description of what that person 'does' or 'is' in their life and is often given as information on the Scenario Cards. A teacher, a student, a husband or a sister would be the 'role' that you would play. The 'character' is what sort of person you are, and that will be described on the Character Cards. You might be a shy person, or you might be arrogant or romantic. You might be an optimist or you might be a leader. That would be your *character*. As I pointed out, a *person's 'character' does not necessarily appear to suit their 'role'*. To clarify things, if we look at the examples above, the 'doctor' would be the role and 'with no interest in humanity' would be the character. So, the judge (role) may be shy (character); the boxer (role) may hate violence (character), etc.

Of course, in reality a person's character is a very complex compilation of character *traits*. An aggressive person can also be romantic and generous at the same time. A person who likes to take control can also be a dreamer and a loner. Everyone is made up of a counless number of interweaving character traits so a one-dimensional description of a person's 'character' is obviously very simplistic. However, for the purpose of these improvisations, the Character Cards are a way of nudging the improviser away from their own behaviour patterns and asking them to take on the behaviour patterns of someone else. Interestingly, what happens is not quite as simple as it might appear, because when someone is given a specific character trait to adopt, what they do is to add it to all their own personal character traits (or highlight a character trait they already possess) and so they end up with a version of themselves which is tilted into a new direction.

Obviously these character descriptions don't tell the whole story about a person, but let's face it, we often use short-cut summaries of character in real life. 'She's so generous.' 'He's a bit of a loner.' 'She's a workaholic.' And although these descriptions are not complete, we know what we mean. A generous person does not always pick up the bill. The loner can sometimes sit and chat to strangers in the pub. A workaholic can have a relaxed Saturday afternoon shopping. But nevertheless, the character descriptions we use still tend to hold true.

Some of the character descriptions on these Character Cards are less clear cut. The 'Searcher' for instance, or the 'Holidaymaker'. What are these descriptions about? Well, these are to be used imaginatively, and by that I mean: people should think about the description and imagine the sort of person that those character traits could be applied to. The 'Searcher' will not always be talking about spiritual matters, but he or she could be the sort of person who feels that something is lacking in their life. Maybe they will have an enquiring, unsettled mind. Maybe the searcher will be gullible and needy. People should think about the description and see what it means to them. Similarly the 'Holidaymaker'. When I use that as a description, I'm thinking about people who are not fulfilled in their work. Who don't even *want* to be fulfilled in their work. The sort of person who has a job in order to earn money which they can then use to relax for a certain amount of the year. But that doesn't mean they always talk about holidays, and it doesn't even mean they don't enjoy their work. Let the improvisers see what a description like that means to them. Let their imagination fill in the details of a person like that.

The 'Fallen star' is a particular favourite of mine because fame is such a part of the common psyche. People want to be on television or have their name in the papers. And now there are so many reality TV shows, more and more people are becoming 'famous for fifteen minutes' as Andy Warhol suggested they would be. And what happens to all those people who have been on *The Jerry Springer Show* or *Big Brother* or *The X Factor* or *The Apprentice*? Of course they will be recognised for a month or two, or a year or two, but what happens when they go back to their un-famous lives? Do they talk about their moment of fame all the time or do they avoid the subject? Does it leave them feeling depressed and worthless or are they proud of their achievement? Has the 'bubble reputation' given them the resolve to do something more worthwhile with their lives or are they continually seeking further recognition? Are they glad to be out of the spotlight or do they feel it was the climax of their life? Who knows? It could be any of those things. As an actor I have seen fame come and go for my friends. I had one particular friend who had massive exposure on television and in the newspapers for a particular period of time. He was in a big US-based television series. While it was being screened in England, he came over to London and we went out for a meal at an expensive restaurant. He was recognised in the street and asked for his autograph. He was greeted by name at the restaurant, and he was given the best table and generally pampered and fussed over. Several years later he was back in London again and, although he had continued to work in various TV dramas and films, he was no longer so 'high-profile'. This time, when we went out to eat, he was treated well because we were spending money, and although people may have recognised his face, they couldn't be quite sure where they'd seen it before. How did he feel about this? How did it make him behave? I can't say he appeared very different, but he must have been *feeling different inside. And it's the 'difference inside' that improvisers should be searching for. Not some external, unsubtle, stereotypical behaviour, but the internal feelings.*

And it's the 'internal feelings' approach to all the cards that people should be exploring. They should read the character description. Let their imagination take flight and see if they can discover a truthful, complex version of a character that is true to the words on the card and true to their life experience at the same time.

Remember. An aggressive person will not be aggressive in all situations, and a shy person can sometimes feel quite confident. A romantic person doesn't fall in love with the first person they meet, and a vain person isn't always checking the mirror.

These cards should be used as subtle suggestions of character. They should 'take people away from themselves', and give them the opportunity to explore different and subtle character traits.

Exercises

Let's All Be Me

Ask everyone to walk around the room, weaving in and out of each other. Then ask them all to do a funny or strange walk accompanied by an extraordinary sound. Pick out someone (e.g. Tom) and say, 'Everyone be like Tom' and they all have to copy Tom's movement and sound. Then say, 'Everyone be like Stephanie,' and they all have to copy Steph, etc. When they have done that a few times move the game on to the next stage. Everyone continues to walk around, weaving in and out of each other with funny movements and sounds but this time someone has to shout out: 'Let's all be me.' At that point everyone has to copy what that person is doing until the next person shouts out: 'Let's all be me,' and everyone has to change what they are doing and copy the new person. And so on and so on. (It's important that they realise that anyone can shout out 'Let's all be me' at any time.)

RATIONALE   *This is a simple game I read in a book of theatre games for children: it's a fun, physical game to warm people up. But at the same time, they are observing other people and copying their mannerisms (however bizarre). And the creation of character through observation of other people is part of the actor's creative process.*

If This Person Was a Tree

Ask everyone to sit in a circle. One person then has to leave the room, and the rest select the name of someone who is left in the circle. When they have done that, the person who has left the room is asked back in, has to stand in the middle of the circle, and try to guess who the group have selected. They do this by asking individuals in the circle questions like 'If this person was a tree, what sort of a tree would they be?' or 'If this person was an item of clothing, what item of clothing would they be?' The person being asked has to think about the person who has been selected and come up with a suitable answer. 'They'd be an oak,' or 'They'd be a T-shirt,' or whatever. The person asking questions has to let the evidence build up until they think they know who it is. They can have three guesses at any time to see if they've got it right.

RATIONALE   *This is a traditional parlour game, but as people think about different sorts of trees or different items of clothing, they think about the qualities and personality traits of the person who has been selected, and as a result it makes them think about character.*

Improvisations

Character Cards Group Improvisation

Divide the group into two halves. One half will watch the other half improvise.

First Group – Turn the Character Cards upside down and ask each person to select one. When they have read their card they should hand it back. Then ask them to perform the following improvisation:

> *They are all residents of a small town or village and are meeting in the church hall to arrange local celebrations for some national event, like the Queen's birthday or something. The event they are organising should involve some sort of parade or show. Maybe a member of the royal family is coming to visit.*

Let the improvisation continue for fifteen or twenty minutes. When they have finished, see if the watching group can guess the characters of each member of the improvising group.

Second Group – Using the Character Cards, select characters as before and then perform the following improvisation:

> *They are all residents of a small town or village and they are meeting on the village green early on a Saturday morning to set up a local fête or fair. They will be stallholders selling home-made biscuits and jam, or they will be setting up simple games like 'guess the weight of the cake' or 'throw hoops over numbers to win the prize'.*

As before, let it continue for fifteen to twenty minutes and then see if the other group can guess each of the characters.

RATIONALE   *These two group improvisations are to introduce everyone to the Character Cards. It's quite a good idea to show them the cards first and let them ask questions before you start, although the character descriptions should be self-explanatory.*

DEBRIEFING   *It is highly likely that they will have overplayed the characters and the guessing will have been easy. It doesn't matter, because it is good for them to mess around with these cards so they become familiar with them before they start using them in a more truthful manner. When the group talks about the experience, it's important for them to understand how to use the cards subtly. (See 'Taking on a New Character' above.)*

⚡ Simple Scenarios with Character Cards

Ask the group to get into pairs. Each pair will then improvise in front of the rest of the group.

The first pair picks one Scenario Card. They read it and, if necessary, decide which role each of them will play (e.g. who is the teacher and who is the student? Or who is the customer and who is the shop assistant?) Then each of the pair picks a Character Card.

It's important to decide the roles before they pick the Character Cards in order to prevent any role decisions being affected by the character they select. As I said earlier, it is sometimes more interesting for a character to have an inappropriate role. For instance, if people were about to improvise 'a teacher and a student' and one of the Character

Cards was a 'Shy person' and the other was a 'Leader', people would tend to give the character of 'leader' to the 'teacher' and 'shy' to the 'student'. However, it could be far more interesting to have a shy teacher talking to a student who always wants to take the lead. These unexpected combinations are always possible and are often closer to real life.

Let each improvisation last for about four minutes and then let another pair have a go.

RATIONALE   *These improvisations are to allow people to practise being more subtle in the way they use the Character Cards. They also give people the opportunity to analyse the way the cards are being used by others in the group and as a result, they present the opportunity for a discussion about subtlety and truth in improvisation*

Session Debriefing

The discussion should be centred on the following questions:

- How did the Character Cards impact on the Scenario?

- How subtly were the Character Cards used?

- What made the improvisations the most truthful?

- Would the improvisation have been different without the use of Character Cards?

- Did the improvisers learn anything new about their characters during the course of the improvisation?

10

Consolidation:

Emotions, Objectives, Activities & Character

How important is this chapter? Emotions, Objectives, Activities, Character. There's nothing new here. We've been through all this. Shouldn't we be moving on to something new?

Well, it's like this. There has been so much to learn so far, that as each new technique is being explored, the previous techniques are often forgotten about and abandoned. What's new is best. Forget yesterday, let's concentrate on today. That's like saying that you can forget about steering when you are learning how to change gear or you can forget about arithmetic when you are studying algebra. Well, you can't. You have to use all the techniques at the same time, you have to be able to use them instinctively. When a painter puts paint on a canvas, that paint becomes part of the composition as a whole. It adds colour. It creates shape and dimension. It's part of texture, of light and shadow. It helps to create an object or it is the object itself. It develops the mood. It affects the emotion. One brushstroke does a number of things, and although the painter has studied how to use paint to perform all these tasks, he or she is not aware of the separate effects that the application of colour will have. Instinct and practice are guiding the imagination, and that in turn is guiding the brush.

Similarly, the improviser must let each of the techniques become part of their instinctive process. They must remember to bring emotion to an improvisation. They must remember to have an objective and an activity. And, of course, they must think about character. And they must be able to do that swiftly, creatively and instinctively. So that is why there is the need for consolidation.

Why not include Trusting Yourself, Being There and Adjusting the Scenario in this session? Why are we not consolidating the sessions that dealt with these things? Well, the purpose of those sessions was slightly different. Those were not techniques as such, they were more like sparks that light the creative fire; they should be practised all the time.

Everyone should work on being able to trust their own creativity at all times; everyone should learn to 'be there', to be in the moment; and, of course, everyone should understand the rules and then adjust the scenario to allow their individuality to shine and do it their way. These are lessons for everyone and should be practised and consolidated all the time.

Applying the Techniques

AT THIS STAGE OF THE IMPROVISATION TRAINING, THE improvisers should focus on the principal components that should be part of any actor's exploration: Emotions, Objectives, Activities and Character. They should be reminded of these and they should be encouraged to apply them each and every time they embark on an improvisation. The improviser is like a juggler who has to practise keeping his clubs in the air until he juggles instinctively. Each of the improviser's components, or techniques, is like one of the juggler's clubs and they have to allow their instincts to keep all the techniques working without having to think about them. And in order to do that, they have to train their instincts by regular practice.

It's time to start using the Complex Scenario Cards. Remember, the improvisers should strive to be just as truthful when they use these, even when the scenarios are not necessarily part of their personal experience. They have probably never been in a successful band arguing about their future direction; they may never have been stuck in a lift or lost in the woods; but it isn't too hard to stretch their imaginations into the truth of these scenarios. They should use their own personal experiences to create an 'emotional memory' of similar feelings and then use that 'emotional memory' to explore unfamiliar situations.

One whole session can be used to practise each of the techniques until they remember to employ them all swiftly and instinctively. That's all they have to do: practise, practise, practise.

(But in fact this repetition doesn't have to be confined to just one session. The improvisers need constant practice to train their instincts and the more they do it, the better.)

Improvisations

Emotions, Objectives and Activities

Divide the group up into pairs and ask each pair to pick a Complex Scenario Card. When they have done that, they should give each other roles if necessary, before picking their Character Cards.

Then ask everyone to think about each of the following:

* An EMOTION *they could bring to the scene*
* An OBJECTIVE *they may have coming into the scene*
* An ACTIVITY *they could be doing during the scene*

Give them a minute or two of thinking time and then ask all the pairs to practise an improvisation at the same time.

When they have done this, ask them to get into new pairs and repeat the whole process again with new Scenario and Character Cards. This time they should be given a shorter time to think about emotions, objectives and activities before they start.

And then again ask them to get into new pairs but give them an even shorter thinking time.

And then again and then again. But for each improvisation they should be given a shorter and shorter thinking time.

Finally, it is worth letting them improvise in front of the group. Let them find new partners and give them only a few seconds of thinking time before they embark on the improvisation.

RATIONALE   *By making the thinking time shorter for each improvisation, they get used to making quick decisions, so the whole process starts to become instinctive.*

Session Debriefing

Discuss how much of a difference it makes to the improvisation when they think about the techniques before they start.

Discuss how adept they are at making decisions before they improvise.

11

Listening

If you listen carefully – I mean really listen – you can hear much more than you think you can. Remember the soundscape exercise in Chapter 4: Atmospheres? There are so many different sounds in any environment: the sounds of your own breathing; the sounds inside the room; the sounds outside the window. There are more sounds than you think there are.

When babies are first born they must be extremely confused. I mean, they've got all these sensory devices to give them some sort of experience of the world around them. They can see things and hear things and smell things and taste things and feel things, and it must be very confusing as their brains receive all these messages at the same time. Nerve endings all over their little bodies will be sending back the feeling of the air, of their Babygro, of their mother's skin, of water in their bath, in fact of everything they touch and everything that touches them. Have you ever noticed how their arms seem to flail about? That's because they are trying to get the feeling of whatever may be nearby. Then there is taste and smell. Some tastes and smells are good and some are bad, but there are loads of them flying around. In the nose, in the mouth. Good ones are obviously the smell of their mother and the taste of milk, but have they distinguished the bad ones yet?

Who can tell?

Then there are those other two fantastic pieces of sensory equipment, the eyes and the ears. These are such highly sophisticated and developed nerve-ending machines that they send messages to the brain which can be interpreted as pictures and sounds. It's pretty amazing.

For the baby these two senses in particular have to be incredibly confusing, because their little brains have got to make sense out of a massive amount of input. And what are those pictures and what are those sounds? And does that picture of a coloured thing shaking about go with that sound of rattling? It's funny to realise that everything we learn about the world comes through these different nerve endings. Without them, people find it hard to survive.

At time goes by, the pictures and the sounds all fall into place, and the baby starts to make sense of the world. The flailing arms hit nearby things, and a sense of distance and perspective is developed. The grasping fingers get hold of things, and the sense of weight and how to control or use objects is learned.

And after they have learned to understand the pictures and the sounds, they start to be aware of language. It takes a lot of listening to realise that the noises that their mother and father make have recognisable patterns that can be used to communicate ideas, but these little kids do it. They listen and listen, and they learn and learn. And then, when they can understand the language, they listen to the words, and it helps them make even more sense of the big wide world they have become part of. Babies and toddlers are great listeners. They realise that the more they listen, the more they understand: the easier life will be. They are no longer struggling to survive on their own; they are being constantly supported by information in the form of words.

Sensory Input

DURING AN IMPROVISATION, PEOPLE ARE BEING SUPPORTED in a similar way. In fact, this session could easily be called: 'Learn from your sensory input,' because, when someone is improvising, there is a load of supportive information coming into their brains through their eyes, nose, ears and sense of touch that could be used as a stimulus for their imagination and lead the improvisation down new paths.

When people are improvising, they are not working in a vacuum. They can gather nourishment from the world around them.

It's like the incident that Dustin Hoffman improvised in *Midnight Cowboy*, and described in the Introduction. He hears something, sees something, allows that sensory input to stimulate his imagination, and effortlessly lets his creativity flow into the scene.

Suppose someone is about to improvise a scene in which they are to be a shop assistant in a shoe shop. Someone walks into the shop and looks around at imaginary shoes. What could they say? 'Can I help you?' or 'Are you looking for something?' Okay, it's a straightforward vocal response to visual input, but there are so many more possibilities. The person improvising the customer is perhaps wearing perfume that the other improviser can actually smell – 'Sorry to be personal, but is that Musk you're wearing?' 'Yes.' 'That so reminds me of my mother.' Etc.

Improvisers should also allow the sights and sounds of the *real world* to impact on them and affect their improvisations. If there is a window in the room, they can look out of it and let what they see become part of *their character's* view of the outside world. If a piano is being played in the room next door, they can imagine that *their character* hears the sound: 'Is that a music shop next door?' 'I used to play the piano myself.' They can make something out of anything they see or hear. They can use it. Feed from it. Enjoy it.

But mainly, of course, *they should listen to what their improvising partner is saying and respond to that.* They'll find loads of stuff there. In his book, *Impro*, Keith Johnstone describes a game called 'Presents', in which a person holds out their hands as if they are giving a gift to another person. That person has to be pleased to receive the gift and then, through mime, they have to make that gift into something interesting. Well, the words that the other improviser says are like gifts. Improvisers should receive these gifts. Be pleased. And then play with them. Make use of them. See if they can do things with the gift of words that their partner never thought possible.

Exercises

Several of these exercises are described in Impro *by Keith Johnstone. They have been adapted to suit this particular session.*

 Meaningless Poses

Ask the whole group to get into pairs, and then have all the pairs work-ing at the same time in different parts of the room. One person, A, strikes a meaningless pose, and the other, B, has to say something to make the pose make sense. For instance, if A were to crouch down with his or her hands on the floor, B could look at A and say: 'On your marks. Get set. Go!' Or if it was B's turn to strike a pose, and B was to stretch upwards on tiptoes with one hand in the air, A could say: 'Do you need help painting the ceiling?' Ask them to take it in turns. Each time, the second person has made sense out of the meaningless pose, the person who has done the pose has to say, 'Thank you.' (For making sense of something meaningless.)

RATIONALE *This exercise is to encourage the improvisers to use visual input as a stimulus for their imaginations, so they get used to using their eyes as well as their ears. Also, by saying 'Thank you', it encourages them to welcome the changes their partners may make, rather than to reject or be suspicious of them.*

 Tangents – It's Funny You Should Say That . . .

With the whole group divided into pairs and all the pairs working at the same time, A has to say a bland phrase and B has to use one word from that phrase and go off at a tangent to it, starting by saying: 'It's funny you should say that . . . ' Then B has to just keep talking for as long as he or she can. (Going off at a tangent means that, as long as one word is used to make the connection, the response can be about anything at all.)

For example, if the first person starts with the phrase:

'I'm tired.'

The second person could say something like:

'It's funny you should say that, because I'm really tired. I was up till 3 o'clock last night because my cat got stuck up a tree and I had to get the fire brigade to get it down . . . and do you know one of the firemen was an old school friend of mine I haven't seen for seven years, and he was telling me that he's exhausted all the time because he has two children . . .'

Having used the word 'tired' as a stimulus for their imagination, the second person should start the exercise again. Please note that this is not a conversation, so they should start with something entirely different, like:

'This floor is dirty.'

And the first person could respond by saying something like:

'It's funny you should say that, because I was supposed to sweep the floor earlier on today, but someone has used the broom to make a flag pole. It's the Queen's birthday today, you know, and we're all supposed to be learning to sing the National Anthem in a three-part harmony.'

Remember, this is an *exercise* not a *conversation*. They should take it in turns to start, and each time they should begin with an entirely new phrase.

RATIONALE   *This exercise is about plumbing the depths of their imaginations and making something out of nothing. It's what Keith Johnstone calls 'over-accepting', and, as such, I should stress that it is not a realistic conversation. Often people don't know what to talk about in an improvisation, so the more they learn to allow themselves to take inspiration from a single word, the more they will trust their instincts, and the more secure they will feel that they'll always have something to say.*

Pounce on a Word

When the group are confident with the previous exercise, you can ask them to turn the exercise into more of a conversation.

With the whole group divided into new sets of pairs and all the pairs working at the same time, A starts by saying a bland phrase and B has to use one word from the phrase and go off at a tangent to it as before. But while B is responding, A has to listen carefully in order to pick out a word, or 'pounce' on a word, and use that word as the stimulus for *their* response. Each time someone pounces on a word they should start with the phrase, 'It's funny you should say that . . . ' The conversation continues with each person listening for a word, pouncing on it, and using it to go off at a tangent to it. For example:

'I've got a new T-shirt.'

'It's funny you should say that, because my mum used to print patterns on T-shirts when she was young. She lived in a caravan in Somerset with two dogs and some chickens.'

'It's funny you should say that, because we had a caravan when I was a kid, but it fell over a cliff and smashed to pieces. Luckily no one was in it, but my whole Lego collection was lost in the sea.'

'It's funny you should say that, because I won a prize for Lego-modelling when I was nine years old . . . '

And so on.

RATIONALE   *The great thing about this exercise is that they have to listen very carefully in order to pick out a useful word to pounce on, and consequently it forces them to listen; and listening is one of the key elements in any kind of acting.*

DEBRIEFING   *They should understand that these exercises are to free their imaginations. They are about listening and responding, and expanding on simple ideas, and, as such, are not particularly realistic. However, they can use what they have learnt more truthfully and sparingly in the following improvisations.*

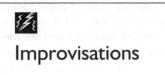

Improvisations

Pick Out a Word

With the whole group divided into pairs, each pair improvises while
the rest of the group watches. Using the Simple or the Complex
Scenario Cards (depending on the progress of the group), each pair is
given a scenario; and then, using the Character Cards, each improviser
is given a character. Each pair then improvises a scene of about four
minutes. During that time, each improviser must listen carefully for
two opportunities to pick out a word and use the phrase, 'It's funny
you should say that . . . ' to go off on a tangent. However, this should
only be done when it is realistic and naturalistic to do so.

RATIONALE   *These improvisations are to allow them to use the exercises
to see if they can be more adventurous in an improvisation without losing
the realism.*

Session Debriefing

For people who are anxious about what to say in improvisations,
this session should make them feel more confident, because
they start to 'feed' from their partners. It should be made clear
to them that, at any time during an improvisation, there will
a number of sensory inputs that can be used to inspire an
improviser's creativity and to move the improvisation into new
areas. All they have to do is to be aware of what is going on
around them, listen to what their partner is saying, and let their
instinct and imagination guide their reactions.

12

Building Together

Working with other people can be difficult and it can be life enhancing. Two independent and creative people can often have tremendous differences of opinion and almost come to blows, and yet two other independent and creative people can pool their resources, share ideas, fuel each other's imaginations and as a result they both can grow and develop.

When I was younger I used to have an old Renault 4. An extremely unpretentious car with very bouncy suspension. One day something went wrong with the clutch and I couldn't get it in and out of gear properly. Now, I'm quite a practical sort of person, but I don't know much about cars.

However, my friend Tony does and he said he'd help me fix it.

All this happened about a week before Christmas. It wasn't that warm, so I suggested that we tow the car over to my mother's house and do the work in her garage. We bought a manual, we bought the new clutch plates, and we set to work.

There was no great rush so we studied the manual. A Renault 4 has a front-wheel drive and in order to get to the clutch you have to lift the engine out of the car; release the front wheels; and remove the gear box. We sorted out our tools and drove off in Tony's car to hire a pulley system. And that was the end of day one.

Next day we set to work attaching the pulley to one of the rafters of the garage; disconnecting all the necessary engine bits; and unbolting what needed to be unbolted. I read the manual and Tony did the work. I made the tea, and Tony made the decisions. I handed him the tools he wanted, he got happily more and more oily. And when it got dark, I held the working light in the right position and he crawled into awkward spaces, spanner in hand. By the end of day two the engine was ready to be lifted out.

Day three, all we had to do to get to the clutch was to dis-connect the front wheels and hoist up the engine. That was when we hit a really major problem. The manual said you needed a special Renault tool to pull the wheels away from the engine. Of course we didn't have one, so we set about improvising. We tried everything. Levers, mole wrenches, spanners, you name it, but the wheels wouldn't budge. Christmas was coming and time was ticking away. Then I suggested we drive round to the local Renault repair garage to see if we could borrow this special tool, and so that was what we did.

I remember this bit well. The mechanic we spoke to was oily and busy. He told us he didn't have the special tool and com-plained about the money that Renault expects mechanics to spend on special tools in order to repair Renault cars and how everything was better in the old days and that you never have this

sort of problems with British cars. We let him say his piece and then Tony asked him how on earth he removed the wheels without the special tool and he said – quote: 'I just hit them with a hammer.'

Brilliant.

So we went back, hit each wheel with a hammer, and like magic they each fell away from the engine. End of day three.

Day four we got to the clutch, pulled it apart, put in the new clutch plates, and started to put the car back together again.

Day five, December 22nd, we finished off the job and by mid-afternoon we started the engine and were ready to drive away.

Only trouble was the new clutch didn't work.

Tony was scratching his head. I was flicking frantically and aim-lessly through the manual and we were fed up. It was raining and it was cold.

Now, I said I don't know much about cars, but feeling like the classic layman, I asked Tony if he thought we could have put the clutch plates in the wrong way round.

Tony paused. He looked at me. He considered this ridiculously naive suggestion. He looked at the manual, wiping oil from the side of his face. He turned to me. He said slowly and carefully: 'Possibly.'

We were depressed. The job had taken us five days. Tony was

heading up north the day after tomorrow. And I still had no car.

'Okay,' he said, 'we'll start again tomorrow and finish the job when I get back in January.'

The next day we got to work again. We didn't speak much because the fun had gone out of the job, but after about an hour I realised that I was anticipating the necessary tools and was ready to pass them over to him at the right time. Pretty soon he didn't even have to ask. Whenever something needed grabbing, pulling, twisting or tugging, there I was at the ready. I was putting the nuts and bolts in sensible piles so they would be at hand when we needed to put everything back together again. Tony smoothly dissected the car parts like a surgeon. I was ready with the pulley system to hoist out the engine. I slipped the hammer in his hand just when he needed it to knock away the wheels. We worked together as a team, and the thrill of mutual understanding and support started to put a glow on the day.

Amazingly, by lunchtime we had the clutch out and sure enough: we had put it in the wrong way round! I felt like a mechanical genius. Tony was delighted that the mistake had been discovered. Continuing to work like an Olympic team, we put everything back together again. The bolts slid into their housings, the engine dropped neatly into place, the wheels went on, all the bits and pieces were fixed where they were supposed to be fixed and by four o'clock we turned on the ignition; pushed in the clutch; engaged the first gear and, smooth as silk, the car moved forwards. We had completed in six hours a job that had previously taken us five days to perform, and we had worked as a team. We had supported each other, we'd responded to each other's needs, and we had anticipated each other's thoughts. Each of us had helped the other and each had taken control when the time was right. It was totally exhilarating.

Mutual Support

A ND THAT'S HOW IMPROVISATIONS WORK BEST. DAY BY DAY, improvisers learn techniques and develop skills, but when they start being able to anticipate each other's thoughts and build together, everything falls into place. They discover that they are never alone in an improvisation. They never have to be in charge. And they never have to feel dominated. They work together.

Improvisers give each other mutual support and they share a common creativity.

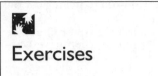

Exercises

Art Gallery Statues

With the whole group divided into pairs and everyone working together, ask one person in each pair to stand in a neutral position and allow the other person to 'sculpt' their body into any physical shape they like so they become a statue. The person creating the statue has to think of what they are 'trying to say as an artist', and they also have to give the statue a title. After a couple of minutes, when all the 'statues' have been created, the people who are the statues have to hold their positions so all the 'sculptors' can walk around the 'art gallery' and talk about each of the works of art. Taking one statue at a time, everyone should examine it, and discuss what they think it may mean and what it might be called. When they have reached some sort of consensus of opinion, the person who made the statue can explain their work of art to the group and tell them its title. Everyone then moves on to the next statue. Having done this, ask the people who were the statues to become the sculptors and vice versa. Then repeat the exercise.

RATIONALE   *This exercise is to encourage people to use what they see as inspiration for what they say. As viewers examine the 'statues', they find much more detail to inspire their imaginations. First, they will have a general impression of the shape and say the 'statue' is about, for instance, 'power', but as they are encouraged to talk in more detail, they will view the position of an arm and say: 'Oh, it's about the abuse of power.' Or they will see how the feet are placed and say: 'It's about a powerful person stamping on a weak person.' And as someone says that, someone else will see the way the 'statue's' eyes are staring and say: 'Look, he hates weak people because they make him feel small.' And so on, as one idea leads to another and the 'meaning' of the 'statue' becomes more and more complex.*

Tableaux

With the group divided into two halves, each half has ten or fifteen minutes to create a tableau that has some sort of message. Each person in the tableau has to know exactly what aspect of the message it is that they represent. So if, for instance, the tableau is 'War', one person could be a soldier and represent violence and another could represent oppression and yet another could represent camaraderie or hunger or death or power. Or even insanity or international politics, or perhaps a bullet missing its target or a boot trampling a field of wheat. There is no limit to what the imagination can create and the body can symbolise. Each half then shows the other half their tableau, and like the 'Art Gallery' exercise, the viewing group have to discuss what they think the tableau is all about and what each person in it represents. When they have drawn a conclusion, the people in the tableau tell them if they were right and then go on to explain all the details.

RATIONALE   *Although this appears to be an exercise in creating physical representations of abstract ideas, the most important part of it is the discussion they have after the tableau has been created when, again, they allow visual input to stimulate their imaginations.*

Boxing

With the whole group divided into pairs and all the pairs working at the same time, ask each pair to stand three metres apart and perform an imaginary boxing match. One person 'throws a punch', and the other has to react as if they have been hit, even though the punch will have been at least two metres from their faces. They don't have to obey the rules of boxing, they can punch, kick, scratch, tickle, etc. etc., but each must physically react to what the other is doing. (It is important to stress that they must never touch each other or even get close to each other.)

RATIONALE   *This exercise symbolises the give and take required during an improvisation. The 'boxers' have to find the right balance between, on the one hand, taking control and, on the other hand, allowing their partner to take control by making the appropriate physical response. Both of them have to keep alert to the continual shift of balance and focus in order to make the 'boxing match' work.*

DEBRIEFING   *After this exercise I often take the opportunity to talk about how this 'boxing match' symbolises the exchange of focus in text-based acting as well as improvisation; where each character has their objectives to play, but at the same time they have to be responsive to the objectives of the other characters. This give and take, this action and reaction, this co-operation and negotiation holds true of any creative partnership. Lennon and McCartney. Gilbert and George. Ant and Dec. Scorsese and De Niro. And many others.*

◧ Expanding Within a Story

Divide everyone into groups of five or six people and ask each group to stand in a circle. With each group working independently, ask one person in each group to say a simple sentence. As in:

'The boy walked down the street.'

Then the next person around the circle has to add something within the sentence. As in:

'The little boy walked down the street.'

The next has to add more, still within the sentence. As in:

'The little boy walked down the busy street.'

And the next . . . As in:

'The little boy walked quickly down the busy street.'

And so on around the circle, continually adding bits of information within the original sentence.

This exercise is not a test of memory, so once everyone in the circle has added their bit to the sentence, the group can stop and start again with a new simple sentence. However, it makes it more interesting if, each time, a different person in the circle starts the exercise off.

RATIONALE   *This exercise is to help the improvisers understand how they can expand a simple idea together and give it complexity and detail. The idea itself doesn't lead anywhere, but as each person adds a little more information it becomes more and more interesting and detailed.*

◼ Confirming the Details – Do You Mean . . . ?

With the whole group divided into pairs and everyone working together,
A says a bland phrase and B responds by saying 'Do you mean . . . ?'
and then inserting an adjective in front of a noun from A's phrase. As in:

> A: 'I came here by bus.'
>
> B: 'Do you mean you came by the red bus?'

Then they start again. This time B says a bland phrase and A has to
insert an adjective, starting with 'Do you mean . . . ?' As in:

> B: 'I love music.'
>
> A: 'Do you mean you love loud music?'

To start with, the exercise should be as simple as that, with each
person taking it in turns to start.

When the group is confident with this, they can take it a step further. B
responds to A's bland phrase by inserting an adjective and then adding
an extension. As in:

> A: 'I've just bought a pair of shoes.'
>
> B: 'Do you mean you bought those black shoes that you are wearing
> right now?'

They should practise that stage of the exercise for a bit, taking it in
turns to start.

The third step, on hearing the bland phrase, is to insert an adjective;
add an extension and then add another extension. As in:

> A: 'I'm going to a club tonight.'
>
> B: 'Do you mean you're going to that brilliant club which has a fantastic
> DJ and everyone has to dress like a character from The Matrix?'

Finally, they can make this exercise more like a conversation by using
the exercise described in the last chapter called 'Pounce on a Word'.
As B responds to A's bland phrase, A listens and picks out a word to
add adjectives and extensions to. As in:

A: 'I've got to work tonight.'

B: 'Do you mean money-making work that you do in the pub on Fridays?'

A: 'Do you mean The Red Lion pub in Acton where you met that girl last October?'

B: 'Do you mean the blonde girl who has a friend that works in Sainsbury's on Saturday afternoons?'

And so on.

RATIONALE   *This is similar to 'Tangents – It's Funny you Should Say That . . . ' as described in the last chapter, but instead of continually going off at tangents and creating new ideas, the original idea is given more and more detail. This encourages improvisers to explore the things they have already created rather than continually striking out in new directions.*

DEBRIEFING   *At this stage the exercise doesn't sound entirely realistic, because it is so forced, but it helps the improvisers in two ways. Firstly, it teaches them to listen to each other and, secondly, it makes them realise that they can use each other's ideas to build complex and detailed stories together. They can build relationships and they can develop characters.*

Improvisations

Gobbledegook Experts

This improvisation requires the use of gobbledegook, so it is best to practise that first. (See 'Gobbledegook' in Appendix: Warm-up Games and Exercises.)

With the whole group divided into pairs, each pair improvises while the rest of the group watches. Introduce the first pair by saying that one of the improvisers is an expert on a particular subject (see the list below) and is going to give a lecture about it, but unfortunately the expert cannot speak any English but has brought a translator (the other improviser) who will translate the lecture for the audience.

As the improvisation starts, the expert has to give their lecture in gobbledegook as if it was a foreign language and the translator has to pretend to translate the gobbledegook into English.

The expert could have:

- *Created an enigmatic work of art using unusual materials*

- *Choreographed an unusual postmodern dance piece*

- *Invented a machine that will change all of our lives*

- *Travelled to remote places and studied the rituals of a primitive tribe*

- *Studied unusual oriental meditation techniques*

- *Created a new sport (a cross between football and fencing perhaps)*

- *Travelled to another planet and explored alien lifestyles*

- *Discovered a new tomb in Egypt with some extraordinary statues and paintings*

- *Built a time machine and travelled to the year 4000*

- *Been asleep for 150 years and has come to tell us about the differences between then and now*

RATIONALE   *The great thing about this improvisation is that both improvisers are continually being inspired by each other. The expert usually uses physical movements along with the gobbledegook in order to make their lecture clear, and the translator watches the movements and makes wild guesses about what is being described. Similarly, as the translator speaks, the expert listens to what is being said and, being inspired by the (often inaccurate) translations, starts to adjust and build their gobbledegook descriptions.*

Session Debriefing

This session explores a major component of any performance that involves more than one person, be it improvisation, text-based scene work, clowning, dancing, making music, etc. etc. And that is mutual support and a shared creativity. In other words, working together constructively, feeding from each other and building together.

When people are improvising, they are often keen to move the improvisation forwards and bring in new ideas, and as a result they leave out a lot of detail on the way. Sometimes one of the improvisers will say something quite interesting but rather than letting it be a source of creativity, it gets more or less ignored because the other improviser is keen to talk about something else. Consequently, as the improvisation progresses it has little or no substance. It may cover a lot of subjects and bring forth a number of ideas, but there is no detail or depth to the subjects or ideas. These exercises encourage the improvisers to add more and more detail to a simple idea, and as a result they learn to build a complex and interesting improvisation together.

13

Releasing the Imagination

Imagination is such an evocative word. Poets are said to have a 'strong imagination'. People, especially young people, are often criticised for having 'no imagination'. I find myself using the word a lot in classes, as in: 'Imagine you are walking in the countryside.' And how often have we heard people say, 'Use your imagination'?

But what is imagination? Is it something we can decide to use when we need to use it and not, when we don't? Like a tool in a toolbox? A carpenter keeps his saw safely in a cupboard and only brings it out when he needs to cut a piece of wood. Is that what the imagination is like? Or is it something that is operating in the background of our brains all the time?

What is imagination?

As I ask myself these questions my mind is roaming and wandering through the vast accumulation of ideas, images, experiences and thoughts that clutter my brain. I'm using my imagination to find an answer to the questions I'm asking myself! So in asking these questions my imagination is searching for a definition of itself. Is that how it works?

Experience and information fill up our brains, and we can tap into them at any time to come up with answers to problems. We imagine. Some people don't think they've got a very good imagination, but what does that really mean? While you are waiting for a bus, you imagine it arriving and you imagine getting on it, you imagine it taking you to work and you imagine getting to work on time; otherwise you wouldn't be waiting. Imagination sifts through our vast range of experience and information, and paints metaphorical pictures in our mind's eye. It trawls the archives of experience and plays fantasy films in the back of our brains. It's doing it all the time. That's why we run from an angry bull. We imagine it tossing us up in the air and goring us with its horns, and we don't want that, so we move away pretty fast. If you didn't use your imagination, you would have no reason to run from the bull. You'd have no reason to wait for a bus. You would not even know why you were standing with other people by a post with a strange sign on top.

Children all have great imaginations. They imagine that their teddy bears and dolls can think and talk. They imagine that they are lions and astronauts and bus drivers. They imagine Father Christmas and the Tooth Fairy. They imagine anything they want, and have no problems with it.

The trouble starts when other people – grown-ups, older brothers and sisters – make children question their imaginative creations. 'Teddy doesn't really talk, that's silly.' 'You can't be a lion. Lions are animals.' 'Believing in the Tooth Fairy is babyish.' And when people say things like that, children start to doubt their own creativity.

These pragmatic statements inhibit the free-ranging, phantasmagorical mental inventiveness that we are all born with, like great big steel shutters clamping down on the windows of our imagination. Consequently, as children get older, they start to doubt the results of their imagination in order to forestall criticism. 'I can't think like this; people will think I'm a baby.' And down comes the shutter. Clomp! 'I can't say that; people will think I'm stupid.' Down it comes again. Clomp! 'I mustn't behave the way I want to behave; people will think I don't like them.' Clomp!

Schiller wrote of a 'watcher at the gates of the mind', who examines ideas too closely. He said that in the case of the creative mind, 'the intellect has withdrawn its watcher from the gates, and the ideas rush in pell-mell . . .' He said that uncreative people 'are ashamed of the momentary passing madness which is found in all real creators . . .'

The imagination is continually being inhibited by the outside forces of mediocrity. Improvisers have to learn to battle these forces and let their imaginations fly. It's not that some people have 'no imagination' or 'a weak imagination', it's that they allow their imaginations to be repressed and restricted by a form of self-censorship.

Imaginations have been	release them and allow them
incarcerated: we need to break	the freedom to take uninhibited
their chains, open the shutters,	flight!

A GREAT WAY FOR IMPROVISERS TO RELEASE THEIR IMAGINA-
tions and explore possibilities is to allow themselves to
be inspired by each other. This session is really a continuation of
the ideas explored in Chapter 12: Building Together, and they
encourage the improvisers to, first of all, listen to each other,
and then secondly, to push their imaginative creativity further
than they would normally allow it to go.

*Improvisers need to take the critical spotlight off themselves in order
to discover how they, or their character, would really behave in any
situation.*

How Far Can They Go?

In my sessions, I am not concerned about improvisers using
inappropriate language, or even allowing their *characters* to make
'politically incorrect' statements. If they are imposing limits on
themselves during an improvisation, then they are creating their
own 'watcher at the gates of the mind', and thereby inhibiting
their imaginations. This is a very tricky area, because, obviously,
I don't want people to get abusive, or to use improvisation as an
excuse to be racist, or to attack minorities, but in my experience,
taking away these restrictions doesn't usually lead them down
inappropriate paths, all it does is empower them, and give them
confidence. However, if any subject, opinion or use of language
becomes a problem during an improvisation, then there is
always the opportunity to discuss these issues with the group
after the improvisation has finished.

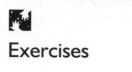

Exercises

Mirrors

This is a familiar game, but it's a good warm-up.

Two people face each other and place their palms a few inches apart. One person has to be the leader and move their hands around while the other has to copy the leader's movements exactly, as if they are a reflection in the mirror. Once they start, the leader can move their whole body, not just their hands, and the 'mirror image' has to follow. It's best to do this slowly so that the person 'reflecting' the movement can keep up.

When one person has been the leader for a bit, let the other person take the lead.

Finally, explain that from now on, neither of them is the leader. Without speaking they must do the same exercise and continually swap the lead. Where one person starts a movement, the other can finish it by taking it in a new direction. Anyone watching them should be unable to tell who is leading at any particular time.

RATIONALE   *This is clearly about concentration and unspoken negotiation. Both people are learning to pick up on the subtle shifts of focus and inter-pretation. They are tuning in to each other's creativity.*

Experts

With the whole group divided into pairs, each pair improvises in turn while the rest of the group watches. The improvisation takes the form of a television interview, or an interview in a lecture theatre, and the only information that the two improvisers are given is their roles. One is the 'interviewer' and the other is the 'expert'. When it starts, the expert has no idea what subject he or she is supposed to be an expert on, in fact, without any discussion, the interviewer starts the improvisation by creating the subject of expertise during the first question. The interviewer should say something like:

'Welcome Mr Brown, it's great to be speaking to you . . . I hear you have invented a method for extracting gold from the scales of goldfish. Can you tell us a bit about how you do it?'

or

'. . . I hear you've discovered a new species of six-legged animals, living in the mountains of Peru . . .'

or

'. . . I hear you've trained an army of ants to bake sponge cakes . . .'

The interviewer can choose any mad combination of ideas they like, and the expert has to start talking about the subject that the interviewer's question has made them an expert on. As the interview progresses, the interviewer must constantly interrupt and add new information to the creation, by picking up on what the expert has said and asking another question that expands on it. The question must never be as simple as 'How do you do that?' Each question should always add more information. So, for instance, if the expert is talking about 'a new species of six-legged animals', and says something like, ' . . . and they have feathers rather than fur . . . ', the interviewer can add to that by asking something like:

'Oh yes, I hear that as a child you used to collect feathers and make models of world-famous buildings out of them. Can you tell us a bit about that?'

At this point, the expert has to go off in a new direction and build on the second question.

It is important that both the interviewer and the expert are continually adding to the story. The interviewer must never sit back and let the expert do all the talking and creating. The interviewer *has* to ask complicated questions that go into new areas, and the expert *has* to expand and develop these new areas.

Although the style or the performance of the interview should be extremely realistic and believable, the subject matter can be as absurd and surreal as they like. The weirder the better as far as releasing the imagination is concerned. If it is entertaining to anyone watching, it should be because the *imaginative verbal creations* are funny, not because the *performances* are clown-like or comedic.

RATIONALE   *During the improvisation, both people have to listen carefully to each other and add to, and change, the story. They both have equal input, and they both learn from each other. In this way they are both opening their imaginations to new ideas and, at the same time, 'feeding' new ideas to each other. They are building together, and taking equal responsibility to create a complex and interesting (albeit ridiculous) conversation.*

DEBRIEFING   *They should understand that the more they listen to each other, the easier it is to share their creativity. Also, they must realise that it doesn't matter if they appear 'silly'. When they say ridiculous things they are opening the shutters and liberating their imagination.*

Preparation for 'Three Bullshitters in a Pub'

It's now time to start combining some of the exercises from this and previous chapters in order to release the improvisers' inhibitions even more, and to really let their imaginations fly.

First of all, ask them to get into pairs, and with all the pairs working at the same time, have them practise 'Tangents – It's Funny You Should Say That . . . ', until they are comfortable with the idea of taking the story off at a tangent. (See Chapter 11: Listening.)

Then ask them to get into new pairs and practise 'Confirming the Details – Do You Mean . . . ?', until they remember how to expand the story from the inside. (See Chapter 12: Building Together.)

Then ask them to practise the following exercise which combines these two techniques and also incorporates 'Experts' (see above).

Banish Politeness

With the improvisers divided into groups of three, and all groups working at the same time in different parts of the room, one person in each group starts the exercise off with a simple sentence, then either of the other two can pounce on a word and do one of the following things:

- They can TAKE THE STORY OFF AT A TANGENT by starting with 'It's funny you should say that . . . '

- They can CONFIRM THE DETAILS by starting with 'Do you mean . . . ?'

- Or they can BECOME AN EXPERT on any aspect of the story so far and talk about their expertise.

Then while the second person is talking, either of the other two can pounce on a word and interrupt by using any of the three techniques above. Then while that person is talking, either of the other two can interrupt and so on.

As the exercise progresses, each person should try to dominate the conversation with their imaginative ideas until it becomes a sort of battle to be the next person to speak. Some people will find it hard to interrupt when someone else is speaking, so they should be encouraged to 'banish' any form of social politeness and nicety and really try to shout each other down. Each person should try to be the one that talks the most, but at the same time, each person should never stop listening to what the others are saying. In fact, they *have* to listen to what the others are saying because that will be the stimulation for their imaginative reactions. They should be asked to continually vary the three forms of reaction.

RATIONALE   *This exercise often becomes a bit of a shouting match as each person tries to interrupt. But at this stage, that is not at all a bad thing, because the competitive nature of the exercise and all the noise in the room tends to free up the more inhibited members of the group. Also, while each person is listening to someone else speak, and trying to find a way in to the 'conversation', their imagination is working overtime.*

DEBRIEFING   *People must not let their notions of politeness inhibit their ability to interrupt someone else. Everyone has to add their own creative contribution. Some people are heavily conditioned not to interrupt when someone else is speaking: but this is just an exercise, not an indication of how to behave in real life!*

Improvisations

Three Bullshittters in a Pub

With the rest of the group watching, ask three people to improvise a scene where they are sitting in a busy pub having a conversation. The sort of conversation where everyone is very lively and everyone is trying to speak at the same time. They should keep the improvisation realistic; they shouldn't be polite; and they should fight for their turn to speak, using the three techniques they have been practising: 'Tangents', 'Confirming the Details' and 'Experts'. Also, as they interrupt, they should each try to 'top' what the others are saying. Three other people from the group can help to create the atmosphere of a pub by joining the improvisation. For instance, they could be a barman and two other customers. However, they should set up the bar to one side and be less noisy than the three main 'bullshitters'. While these other three are creating the background atmosphere, they can practise the exercise themselves, so when it is their turn to be the three bullshitters, they will have had a bit of a warm-up.

RATIONALE   *This improvisation is to give everyone ample opportunity to let their imaginations run wild. It is very close to the way conversations sometimes go when people actually are in a pub, although a lot of these imaginative inventions will probably be more bizarre than realistic. But as long as the* performance *or* style *of the improvisation is naturalistic, it doesn't matter that they may be talking exaggerated nonsense. In fact, it should be encouraged, because the whole point is to push this exercise to the maximum. Having taken things to an extreme, they can always pull back to more realistic inventions at a later date.*

Session Debriefing

By now, people should be able to concentrate on listening to each other for anything that can inspire or stimulate their imagination. At the same time they should be able to let their imaginations fly without self-censorship. Two things are happening here. The more they concentrate within the scene, the less they are likely to want to try to 'entertain' an audience and the more truthful they will become. At the same time they will realise that there is a lot of food for their imagination if they keep focused within the scene. Add to that the notion of 'being there' and not having to do anything except concentrate on the truth of a situation and just respond naturally to whatever is said or whatever happens, and they will be starting to improvise in a way that is useful for exploration and discovery. Creative improvisation. Improvisation for actors!

14

Re-incorporating

I haven't talked much about jazz so far, and, given that jazz is notorious for – even dependent on – improvisation, then it's clearly a big oversight. In fact, improvisation is the *raison d'être* for jazz. Improvisation and jazz go together like peaches and cream, like Laurel and Hardy or like a rhythm section – the drum and the bass of jazz. Each can operate independently but the combination is usually greater than the sum of the parts.

Jazz, strangely enough, has not always been improvised. In the early days it was orchestrated and carefully written down, but the trouble was that not all the musicians could read music, so they had to play by ear and memory. The harmonies and syncopated rhythms were difficult to remember, variations to the prescribed notes began to slip in, and those variations sounded great. Actually, Jelly Roll Morton, who claims to have invented jazz, would fine the musicians in his band if they played a wrong note. Where's the jazz in that? And even now you can hear that his recordings are less exciting than, say, the early recordings of Louis Armstrong.

Over a few short years Louis Armstrong took popular dance music into a whole new area by using daringly improvised instrumental solos and unrehearsed, again, often improvised, vocals. If you listen to the Hot Five and Hot Seven recordings of 1925 to

1928 in chronological order, you can hear the real birth of jazz as we know it. These are interesting recordings for a number of reasons. For a start, the band only existed in the studio. They never played live gigs together (although, some of the musicians played with Louis in King Oliver's Creole Jazz Band). Louis Armstrong was twenty-four when he started the Hot Five recordings, so he was bursting with creative ideas. Lil Hardin, his wife, was on the piano, Johnny Dodds on clarinet, Kid Ory on trombone, Johnny St Cyr on banjo, and of course Louis played the cornet, which he had learned at reform school when he was just twelve years old.

The first Hot Five recordings were more or less ensemble pieces. All the musicians played at the same time throughout most of each number, in a complex inter-weaving of harmony and rhythm. For the next few recordings, solos were given to Johnny Dodds and Lil Hardin – possibly because the clarinet and the piano were the quietest instruments in the band, and they couldn't be heard proper-ly when everyone else was playing. After all, these were acoustic rec-ordings. No electric amplification was involved at all. And the cornet and trombone were much louder brass instruments that could always be heard above the mix with a bit of extra blowing.

Pretty soon everyone wanted their own solo. Accompanied by just the piano and the banjo,

each member of the band would take a solo 'break' and improvise around the main tune. The band would only play together for the opening few bars to establish the melody, and then not again until the last chorus, when everyone played in a frenzy of harmonic interweaving and syncopated rhythms. It was exciting, competitive and joyful.

As I said, no electrical amplifica-tion was involved. For these early acoustic recordings the musicians all crowded round a huge metal horn which collected the sound, funnelled the vibrations down a tube to a vibrating needle, which cut the oscillating groove straight onto the wax disc. It was tight, rhythmical dance music, and it was recorded as it was being played. It must have been quite scary and very exciting.

People say that Louis Armstrong invented 'scat' singing (singing without using proper words) in 1926 when he was recording 'Heebie Jeebies' and dropped the piece of paper which had the words on it. Who knows? 'Be-duh – Beep – Bup – Bee-Bup Dee Dah-Dee Dah.' Without the lyrics to hand, he started singing words that don't really make much sense. He sings things like 'I've got the Heebies,' and 'Don't you know it, bee duh – bah bah don't feel blue.' And then he sings, 'Papa's got the heebie jeebies dance,' before he throws caution to the winds, doesn't bother with real words at all and just makes 'Be-dup-bob' sounds until the end of the last chorus, when he sings the chorus line about 'Papa's got to do the heebie jeebies dance' again.

Whatever the truth behind the legend, it's a joyous recording and obviously a spontaneous, confident, dangerous and totally infectious improvisation. You hear it once, and you want to hear it again immediately. We love to repeat things we are familiar with. That's why songs have choruses. There's something comforting about the same words turning up at regular intervals during a song. Not only do we love to hear them but singers love to sing them. It reminds them of the main theme of the song and gives them focus.

The chorus generally draws everything together and sometimes the repeated words are used in a new context to make us think.

Jazz musicians do the repetition thing all the time, not just with the notes of the chorus. They may go off on improvised flights of fancy, but every so often they re-incorporate a piece of the tune they've played before. They repeat an inspired piece of musical improvisation. And somehow this repetition, or re-incorporation, endows the music with solidarity or wit or gravitas or drama or romance. It's a powerful device. It stimulates the memory and powers the imagination.

Why Re-incorporate in a Non-Performance Improvisation?

KEITH JOHNSTONE WRITES ABOUT RE-INCORPORATION IN his book on improvisation: 'The improviser has to be like a man walking backwards. He sees where he has been, but he pays no attention to the future.' I like that thought. He then goes on to describe how much pleasure the audience gets from re-incorporation. 'Sometimes they even cheer!' he says. 'They admire the improviser's grasp.'

That's all true. And as far as Performance Improvisation is concerned, admiration and laughter are obviously an important part of the entertainment, but since we're not concerned with audiences and entertainment here, why should we be concerned with re-incorporation at all? As I keep saying, these improvisations are about exploration and discovery and, as such, there should be no thought of entertaining an audience.

Well, for a start, improvisers need to build on the characters and relationships they have already invented during an improvisation, so for that reason it's important to be 'like a man walking backwards'. And secondly, keeping mentally alert and searching for moments to re-incorporate keeps improvisers focused and in tune with the truth of their creation. It's easy for them to let their thoughts wander away from the reality of an improvisation. There are a million distractions: seeing other people out of the corner of their eye can spoil their concentration; remembering who their improvising partner really is can make their minds wander; something their partner says can distract them from the fragile fantasy they have created. *But when they continually think back on the improvisation so far, it can help them stay concentrated and thus avoid distractions.*

It's funny, but an improviser not only has to be like a man walking backwards, but he or she also has to be like an absorbent sponge, sucking up every clue. An improviser also has to be an impostor taking on another personality; a boxer responding to his opponent's moves and waiting for the right moment to take control; a psychiatrist delving into someone else's psyche; and a poet distilling and controlling dangerous emotional depths. And not only that, the improviser has to be doing all these things at the same time like a juggler. In fact, the improviser has to be all these things *and* be a juggler. Amazing what human beings can do, isn't it?

Exercises

Nouns

Provide everyone with plenty of scrap paper and some felt-tip pens. Ask each person to take four pieces of paper, write a noun clearly on each piece and then place them in a pile with everybody else's, face down in the middle of the room. When they have done that ask them to get into groups of four.

Two people from each group of four will do a simple improvisation – a chat about their holidays, or what happened at the weekend – and the other two will be their helpers. Before the improvisation starts, ask the helpers to each pick up four random pieces of paper from the pile but to keep the writing hidden. Then ask each of the helpers to stand in the eye-line of one of the improvisers in their group, and let the improvisers start their conversation. After the improvisation has been running for about a minute, one of the helpers should hold up a piece of paper, and the improviser who can see it has to incorporate that noun into their improvisation smoothly and naturally. After the first one, the helpers can then show any of their nouns at any time, and the improvisers have to keep incorporating or re-incorporating the words. The nouns should not be shown too fast or it all becomes a bit silly.

RATIONALE   *This is a fun game to get them started on the idea of re-incorporation. It's a game that forces them, first of all, to incorporate something into their improvisation that they wouldn't normally have thought of and then it forces them to re-incorporate the same thing later on in the improvisation.*

Re-incorporating Round the Circle

Ask the group to stand in a circle and make up a story which progresses round the circle, with each person adding a phrase when it comes to their turn. (See 'Story Around the Circle, a Phrase at a Time' in Appendix: Warm-up Games and Exercises.) However, before they start, tell them that on a given signal, like a clap of the hands or a beat of a drum, the next person to speak has to re-incorporate something from an earlier part of the story. Of course the story should be given time to establish itself, but then the signals can happen quite often, so that people are continually thinking about the earlier part of the story in order to be able to re-incorporate.

RATIONALE   *This exercise encourages them to remember what has been said before. They have to keep as much of the story in the forefront of their minds as possible, so they can re-incorporate swiftly and smoothly on the given signal.*

DEBRIEFING   *At this point it's worth discussing how easy they found re-incorporation and what difference it made to their concentration. Did they enjoy revisiting bits of the story or did they want to move on? Was it exciting? Was it difficult? What did they get out of it?*

Improvisations

Re-incorporating Improvisations

With the whole group divided into pairs, each pair improvises while the rest of the group watches. Using the Simple or the Complex Scenario Cards and the Character Cards, ask each pair to improvise a scene of about four minutes. Tell them that after a couple of minutes they will be given a signal (a handclap or the beat of a drum), at which point one of the improvisers has to talk about something that was mentioned earlier in the scene. On a second signal, the other person has to do the same thing. These improvisations should be entirely truthful and naturalistic and the two re-incorporations should be introduced smoothly and effortlessly, so that if someone who wasn't part of the group was watching, they would have no idea that this particular technique was being employed.

It's important to allow each improvisation to be properly established before the signal to re-incorporate is given, otherwise there isn't much material for them to revisit.

RATIONALE   *Although the use of a signal telling them when to re-incorporate can take their minds off the reality of the improvisation, while they are waiting for the signal they have to concentrate on the scene, and remember what has been said. The more they repeat these improvisations, the more they get used to finding their own points of re-incorporation, and in the end there will be no need for any kind of signal. They will just do it instinctively.*

Session Debriefing

This session is to encourage the improvisers to remember what they have created so far and to use that as food for their imagination. It's also about keeping their focus and concentration within the confines of the improvisation and not continually trying to break new ground. At any point during an improvisation, the things they have said before can be a valuable source of inspiration.

15

Incidents

Things happen to us all the time that we have no control over, and yet we still have to carry on with the details of our lives. I'm talking about the times when we're trying to be cool, and we suddenly get a bout of hiccups for no reason at all; or the time when we're trying to chat up that special other person, and we spill coffee all over ourselves. These incidents can happen without warning, but when they do we often try to carry on without drawing too much attention to them. We try to gulp down the hiccups, or we surreptitiously hold our breath. We say the coffee stain won't matter. We continue the conversation, but there are changes to the mood. Subtle adjustments to our behaviour.

I was filming a commercial one time, and I had woken up feeling quite ill. Of course I forced myself to go to work: you can't take the day off on an occasion like that. The money for one day's filming can be quite substantial, and there is no chance of postponing the shoot for another day: the studio has been booked; the crew have been booked; you've been booked. Everything is set, and time is money. So, although I was feeling rough, I got myself ready, and went to work.

In this commercial I was the main character, and I had to be jolly and enthusiastic about the product. Of course there is a lot of sitting around during filming, but there is also an atmosphere of focus and activity from everyone. Since no one there knew anything about me, I realised that if I could just manage to keep myself to myself and be pleasant enough when I was needed, they would just think I was a quiet sort of guy. It worked well. I got on with the job. Everyone else got on with their jobs and there was the usual feeling of calm yet efficient forward-moving, time-conscious activity.

I did my best, but I was feeling awful.

No one had any idea that I was ill, until late in the morning, right in the middle of yet another 'take' – and these commercial takes are very short, somewhere between 5 and 10 seconds – I just passed out. One minute I'm acting enthusiastic and jolly about the product, and the next I'm lying on the floor, out cold. Everyone was pretty shocked.

And then they were concerned about my welfare.

And then they realised that we were halfway through the day, and they had to finish the shoot with an ill actor. That was when they got really worried.

However, they were on the horns of a dilemma: if they didn't do anything about my illness, I might be in such a bad way that they couldn't finish the shoot, but on the other hand, they couldn't send me to a doctor or a hospital, because I was the only actor and without me they couldn't finish the shoot either.

So they didn't call a doctor. What they did was carry on filming with the same efficiency and professional haste, while at the same time they continually enquired after my health, made me cups of tea, gave me aspirins, asked me if I wanted to lie down, etc. etc. I've never had so much attention in my life.

But the point I'm trying to make here is that when I passed out, it was an incident that I had no control over, and although it stopped the shoot for a minute or two, it didn't really stop our main activity. We still made the commercial. I acted. The director directed. The crew crewed. We all did what we had been doing before and we talked about the same professional things we had talked about before, but mixed in with all this, there was an underlying sense of concern about my welfare. This personal incident altered things, but it didn't entirely change the scenario.

Then there is the other kind of incident that actually does change things. If this first example is of a 'personal' incident, then the next set of examples to consider are 'external' incidents. The downpour that stops a cricket match. The earthquake that rocks a building. The 'Person from Porlock' who interrupts Samuel Taylor Coleridge and prevents him from finishing 'Kubla Khan'. These external incidents have a big impact on the established normality.

My dad told me how confused and helpless he felt when, during the Second World War, he discovered his office had been bombed. Apparently he took the commuter train up to the City as per usual, and when he arrived at his office, the building just wasn't there. It was a pile of rubble. Nothing left at all.

Some of his fellow workers arrived about the same time, and no one knew what to do. They milled about for a bit, and then they all went home. My mother said that Dad got quite depressed. No one had mobile phones in those days, and anyway, Dad didn't know anyone he could call. His boss hadn't given him his home phone number. All my dad could do was to stay at home and wait for someone to get in touch with him.

I don't know how this resolved itself because I never asked, but it certainly changed things on the day it happened. No workplace. No work. He had to do something else. Knowing my dad he probably spent the next few days gardening.

So whereas 'personal' incidents alter the mood of the scenario, 'external' incidents can change it altogether.

Making Something Happen

THE GREAT THING ABOUT AN IMPROVISATION IS THAT THE improvisers themselves can alter things whenever they want. They can make things happen. If the improvisation appears to be stuck, or it doesn't feel as if it's going anywhere, one or other of the improvisers can create an incident that will alter the mood or modify the scenario quite dramatically. And if both the improvisers are working in harmony, then the changes that one person creates will be incorporated and embellished by the other.

By making something unexpected happen during an improvisation, an improviser can stimulate the creativity of both themselves and the person they are working with.

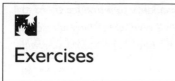

Exercises

Missing

With the whole group working at the same time, but with each person working on their own, talk them through the following solo improvisation:

'It's a warm evening in late summer, and you are walking home after having been on holiday. Although you were on your own when you were away, you had a great time and you feel relaxed and happy. You get to your house or flat and let yourself in. Imagine that you live alone, but apart from that, everything is as it really is for you in your own life. Because you've been away, the curtains are drawn and the room smells musty. You open the curtains to let the light in. You open the windows and let in the air. Do what you would do. Unpack your clothes . . . Make a cup of tea . . . Run a bath . . . Whatever. But make sure you put on the television so you can catch the news. When you turn the television on, it's one of those programmes where they show clips of pop groups from twenty years ago. As you watch, you realise that one of the dancers in the studio is a very young . . . ' (pick the name of their dance teacher, or some appropriate person that they all know.)

Let them react to that and then continue:

'You then flick channels to a news programme. The newsreader is saying something about a missing person. Nobody has heard anything from this person for over a week. Everyone is worried. Then a picture of the missing person comes on to the screen and it's a picture of you! You are the person who is missing!'

Again, let them react. When they start reaching for the phone, tell them that no one is answering, or the number is engaged. Get them to try another number. Still no answer. Let the panic build. Ask them to make three or four phone calls, but absolutely no one replies. Eventually suggest that they call the police. Let them do that and only when the police answer are they able to explain their problem.

RATIONALE   *This exercise uses several incidents to introduce them to the concept that, even when they are on their own, something like seeing a teacher on TV or discovering that they have been reported missing will change the mood.*

DEBRIEFING   *This is the beginning of a session about how to react to unexpected incidents or changes. How did they respond? How did the newsflash change things? How did their emotions alter as they tried in vain to contact someone over the phone? How did they feel when they eventually got through to the police?*

🔳 Personal Incident Exercises

1. House of Cards

With the whole group working at the same time, but with each person working on their own, ask them to mime building a house of cards. Then talk them through this exercise in the following way:

'Concentrate on the task and place each imaginary card on top of the others . . . Be careful . . . Lean them together in pairs . . . Sense the fragility of the construction as you try to stop your hands from trembling . . . Hold your breath . . . Move with utter caution and control.'

And when they've done that for a minute or so, and they are really concentrating, say:

'You suddenly sneeze and the whole structure crumbles to the floor.'

I usually clap my hands on the word sneeze to give it a distinct emphasis. Then I ask them to start building again.

DEBRIEFING   *After this exercise, have a discussion with the group: How did they behave? What happened?*

2. Business Lunch

Ask the group to divide themselves into pairs and then have all the pairs working at the same time. (For this and the next exercise, it's better if the pairs are mixed gender.) Ask them to decide who is A and who is B. A wants to impress B and is taking B out to lunch.

Ask them to decide what that situation could be. Maybe A is an actor taking his agent out for a meal. Maybe A has a new boyfriend and is taking the boyfriend's father out for a bonding lunch while the boyfriend is at work. Whatever they decide, B should be someone important in A's life.

Once they have decided what the situation will be, gather all the As together and tell them, secretly, that, when you give a signal (a hand clap or beat of a drum), they must suddenly realise they have left their wallet at home but they must still try to continue the conversation and the meal. Send them back to their partners and start all the pairs improvising at the same time. After a couple of minutes, give the signal for the incident, allow the changes to unfold and then let the improvisation to continue for a minute or two more before you end it.

DEBRIEFING   *Again, discuss with the group:*

How did the incident affect their conversation? How did A cope? How did B feel? Did B know something was wrong?

3. Blind Date

In the same pairs, say that this time the improvisation is two people on a blind date, having a meal together. Then gather the Bs together and tell them secretly that when you give a signal (a handclap or beat of a drum), they should imagine that they start to feel ill. They should let the illness make them feel queasy, but still struggle on with the blind date for a minute or two, until they eventually faint. Thirty seconds after fainting, they should 'come round' and try to carry on with the lunch and the conversation. As before, start the improvisation, give the signal after a couple of minutes, allow the incident to unfold and then let the improvisation continue for a minute or two longer before you end it.

DEBRIEFING   *This is a more worrying incident for A, because he or she doesn't know if B is going to recover from the fainting fit. Discuss with the group:*

What did A do when B was lying on the floor? How did A feel at that time? How did the mood of the blind date change after the incident?

4. Birthday Party

Divide them into small groups and ask them to improvise a party. When the parties are underway, secretly tell one person from each group to bring in an imaginary cake and start singing 'Happy Birthday'. Just as they are about to put the cake down, tell them they should trip over something and drop the cake on the floor. Let the improvisation continue after the accident in order to see how everyone reacts.

DEBRIEFING   *This is funny. Everyone is usually shocked when the cake is dropped, but then they all have a laugh, so it's not such a disaster. Actually it's rather bonding for the partygoers.*

RATIONALE   *The previous four exercises introduce them to the idea that they can make something unexpected happen during a scene. They also demonstrate how these unexpected personal incidents can enhance, rather than destroy, the improvisation.*

Improvisations

Personal Incident Improvisations

With the whole group divided into pairs, each pair improvises while the rest of the group watches. Use the Simple or the Complex Scenario Cards and the Character Cards to set up the scene in the normal way, but before they start, give them a few seconds so that each person can secretly decide on a personal incident that could happen to them during the improvisation: a nosebleed; something in the eye; an attack of cramp; a lost contact lens. Something like that. Tell them that on a given signal (a handclap or beat of a drum) either of them has to make their incident happen. They should both try to carry on with the scene for a while and then, whenever they want, the other person should make *their* incident happen. After that, let the improvisation continue even longer to see what happens.

RATIONALE   *This improvisation allows them to practise the technique in a reasonably realistic way. It also gives them the opportunity to think up their own incidents and have a certain amount of choice when to deploy them.*

DEBRIEFING   *These improvisations can get quite chaotic. Of course it's unlikely that, in the normal course of events, someone will get something in their eye at about the same time that someone else stubs their toe, but remember . . . it's not impossible! The improvisers should be reminded that, however disrupting the incidents are, their reactions should still be as realistic and truthful as possible.*

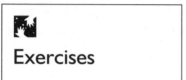

Exercises

External Incident Exercises

1. Revising for an Exam

With the whole group working at the same time but each person working on their own, ask them to imagine that they are revising for a very important exam which takes place tomorrow. They must really concentrate on the job in hand and feel the pressure of last-minute revision. After they have been revising for a minute or so, suddenly tell them that there has been a power failure, the lights have all gone out and they can't see a thing. Let them continue for a minute or two 'in the dark'.

DEBRIEFING   *As with the Personal Incident Exercises, have a discussion: How did things change? What did they do? How did they feel?*

2. Having a Picnic

Divide the group into pairs, and have all the pairs working at the same time in different parts of the room. Ask them to imagine that they are having a picnic in the countryside. After a couple of minutes or so, tell them that it has started to rain. Again, let the improvisation continue for a minute or two to see how they cope.

DEBRIEFING   *Discuss:*

What did they do? How did the pace of the scene change? How did the incident affect their mood?

3. Watching Football on TV

Divide everyone into groups of four and have all the quartets working at the same time in different parts of the room. Ask them to imagine that they are football supporters who have got together to watch an exciting football match on television. It's five minutes before the end of the match and the score is one all. Let them improvise for a minute or so and then tell them that the television breaks down and the screen goes blank. (As before, I clap my hands as I tell them that, in order to give them a distinct moment to respond to.) Let the improvisation continue for a minute or two to see what happens.

DEBRIEFING   *Discuss:*

How did they feel? How did the atmosphere change? How did they respond?

RATIONALE   *The previous three exercises introduce them to the idea that they can make an unexpected external incident happen during a scene. As with the personal incidents, they demonstrate how unexpected changes can really make a scene come alive and head in new directions.*

4. Going for a Drive

With different groups of four, ask them to imagine they are going for a drive through the countryside. Let the improvisation continue for a couple of minutes and then tell them that they are in the middle of nowhere and that they have run out of petrol. When they get out of the car to try to solve the problem, tell them that it's starting to rain. Let them deal with that, then tell them that lightning strikes a tree and it falls on the car. Let them deal with that, then tell them that a herd of cows has escaped and is coming down the road. Let them deal with that, then tell them that an alien spaceship has landed in the next field.

Let them deal with that, and then stop the improvisation. (You can make up any external incidents you like for this, of course.)

RATIONALE   *This improvisation can get quite crazy, but however extreme the incidents become, the improvisers should still have truthful and realistic reactions. I always like to end with the alien spaceship to see if they can still be realistic in a fantasy situation. Soon they will be moving on to the Extreme Scenario Cards and this is an introduction to the kind of fantasy that they will have to explore when they use them.*

DEBRIEFING   *Identify the difference between a Personal Incident – when something happens to them; and the External Incident – when something happens nearby that will affect them.*

See how they responded to the incidents; particularly discuss the alien spaceship. Were they able to imagine how they might react if that really happened?

Having used that extreme fantasy incident, you should tell them that, although the incidents they choose during the rest of the session can be as extreme as they like, they must stay within the realms of known reality (i.e. not aliens or ghosts or goblins, etc.).

⚡ Improvisations

⚡ External Incident Improvisations

With the whole group divided into pairs, each pair improvises while the rest of the group watches. Use the Simple or the Complex Scenario Cards and the Character Cards to set up the scene in the normal way, but before they start, give them a few seconds so that each person can secretly decide on an external incident that could happen during the improvisation: an earthquake; lightning strikes; something catches fire; a mad dog attacks. Ask them to improvise as normal, but tell them that after a couple of minutes they will be given a signal (a handclap or beat of a drum), at which point one of them has to make their incident happen. The other person can make their incident happen any time after that.

Before they start you should explain that, when they make the incident happen, it's important that the other improviser knows what the incident is. This is the only occasion I'm prepared to bend Rule 5 (see the Introduction) – 'Don't try to explain or clarify anything to whoever might be watching; just be truthful' – because if the other improviser doesn't know what your imagined external incident is, then they can't join in, and it will be confusing. A brief conversational explanation can help move things on sensibly. Something like: 'Oh dear, it's started to rain really hard,' or 'Did you feel that earthquake?' or 'Help me. This dog won't let go of my ankle.'

Once the incidents have been established, let the improvisation continue and see what happens.

RATIONALE *As with the personal incidents, these improvisations can be quite chaotic, but as long as the improvisers remain truthful to their invented incidents, and don't start messing around, then the results can be quite amazing. As they explore dangerous and exciting scenarios, they will find that they are able to imagine the reality of any situation they like, be it aliens, flash floods, stampeding elephants or ghosts, etc.*

It's also worth discussing how these techniques can be used to bring life back to an improvisation that seems to be stuck. Sometimes an improvisation seems to be going nowhere, but if 'an angry bull suddenly appears', strangely enough, things can get a little more interesting.

Session Debriefing

This session is about being inventive and making things happen, but it is also about encouraging improvisers to accept the inventions and changes that their partner brings to a scene. Although they may feel they have got the measure of an improvisation, and they may be enjoying the direction it is taking, they should always welcome any changes that another improviser initiates, and accept these incidents as stimulating and exciting challenges to their creativity.

16

Interruptions

Have you ever been at a party and you are in mid-flow telling a relative stranger about a fascinating, amusing, poignant, romantic time of your life, and you are just getting to the nub of the story, when a long-lost friend of the relative stranger you are talking to bounces over and starts shrieking about how fabulous it is to see them again, and you get introduced, and you say 'Hi,' and you are desperate to finish your story, but neither the stranger nor their friend seems to be interested, but you try to do it anyway, and the story loses all its entertainment value?

Oh you haven't? It's just me then.

What about a time when you are with some friends, and you have all just started to watch a game of football, when the plumber arrives two hours late to repair the washing machine, and wants to talk to you about his nightmare traffic problems, and you miss an early goal, and while everyone cheers, he tells you all the reasons he hates football, and won't stop?

Or how about that time when you are shopping with a friend and she's just about to help you choose between three items of clothing, when her new boyfriend turns up unexpectedly and they can't take their eyes off each other, and neither of them are interested in your appearance anyway, so you have to ask a shop assistant to help you choose?

We get these unexpected interruptions all the time. And when they happen we just have to deal with them and carry on. We can't just say, 'Sorry, we were in the middle of something else and you've broken our concentration.'

And anyway, sometimes these interruptions can turn out to be more interesting than the things they interrupt. The person who interrupted your story at the party could turn out to be a gorgeous, undiscovered soul-mate. The washing machine repair man could be the long-lost brother you never knew you had. The shop assistant could be from market research and wants to present you with a large cash prize!

Anything could happen.

The Objective Mind

ONCE PEOPLE HAVE WORKED ON ALL THE TECHNIQUES described in this book, they will be able to use their acting skills to produce interesting and truthful improvisations in any workshop or rehearsal situation in which they may find themselves. They will be able to explore character and relationship in a creative fashion to enlighten and inspire themselves, other improvisers, session leaders or directors.

However, improvisations can be made even more interesting and informative by the input of other people. If, for instance, another improviser is watching a scene and thinks it needs a bit of help to get it out of a rut, they can join in, and introduce new and unexpected elements. If a director or teacher wants to take a scene in a new direction without interfering with the flow, they can ask someone else to enter the improvisation as a new character or a person with a particular task.

In fact, scene interruptions can introduce elements that people who are busy improvising could never have dreamed of. It's difficult for them to think up changes to a scene when they are concentrating on the thought processes of the character they are playing; trying to create a truthful scenario; and working with the inventiveness and imagination of another improviser. *Sometimes an objective eye sees more clearly what an improvised scene needs to make it more interesting, to enhance its reality or to make it come alive.*

But it's important for improvisers to keep an open mind to outside ideas and to be receptive to external contributions.

They need to embrace the creativity of other improvisers who may suddenly arrive with unusual characters and unexpected ideas. They need to allow a scene to travel in unpredictable and exciting directions. They need to welcome change and go with the flow!

Exercises

 Joining In

1. Intimate Meal

With everyone divided up into groups of three and all the groups working at the same time, ask two people in each trio to improvise a scene where they are having an important conversation in a restaurant. Before they start they should give themselves a relationship of some sort, and decide why they are there. After it has been running for a couple of minutes, ask the third person from each group to join the scene as an overattentive waiter who won't leave them alone or an old school friend who happens to be in the restaurant and wants to talk about old times.

2. Plans for the Future

With the same groups of three, ask them to choose a different person to be the interrupter. The other two should then start an improvisation where they are a couple of friends in the park, trying to plan something – an important party, a holiday or a night out. After the improvisation has been running for a couple of minutes, ask the other person to arrive and try to borrow some money from them, or to try and get back a book they lent to one of them last week.

3. Relationship Problems

Again, with the same groups of three, the third person becomes the interrupter. Ask the other two to be flat-sharers discussing the problems of their relationship. After a minute or two the third person can arrive as a neighbour wanting to borrow some sugar, or they could be a person on the phone trying to sell double glazing. (If someone wants to interrupt by being a phone call, all they have to do is to say 'Ring ring . . . ring ring . . . ' until someone in the improvisation realises what is happening and mimes answering the phone.)

RATIONALE   *These three improvisations give everyone a chance to be the interrupters, and at the same time they give everyone two opportunities to deal with interruptions.*

DEBRIEFING   *At this stage it's a good idea to have a discussion about their experiences during these improvisations. Some people find it annoying to have, what appears to be, a perfectly reasonable improvisation spoiled by a random person, but if they learn to accept these interruptions, then their improvisations will become more exciting and unpredictable.*

⚡ Improvisations

⚡ Interruptions

With everyone divided up into groups of three and all the groups working at the same time, ask two people to start an improvisation using the Simple or Complex Scenario Cards and the Character Cards in the usual way. After a couple of minutes have the third person interrupt the improvisation with one of the following objectives:

- *You want them to come to see the circus parade that is coming down the street*

- *You want to ask them to help you get a pregnant woman to hospital*

- *You want to get them to help you push a car that won't start*

- *You want to strike up a conversation because one of them is an old boyfriend or girlfriend*

- *You want to convert them to a new religion or philosophy*

- *You want to sell them something*

- *You've lost your wallet and you want them to help you find it*

- *You want them to help you translate a letter that is written in French*

- *You want to tell one of them that they have won the lottery*

- *You've lost your dog and you want them to help you find it*

Tell the person interrupting that they mustn't give up too easily. The other two improvisers have to see if they can deal with the interruption without losing sight of the original scenario.

With people in the same groups of three, try two more scenarios, so that each person can have the opportunity to be the interrupter.

RATIONALE   *This time the interrupters have strong objectives to achieve, so the improvisers have to stay really focused on their improvisation. They should be learning to welcome these changes, and they should recognise that these interruptions add colour and depth to a scenario.*

DEBRIEFING   *How did the interruption change the scene? Did it stay truthful? As improvisers, were they pleased or annoyed with the interruption? As characters, were they pleased or annoyed with the interruption? Did they learn anything about their characters?*

Group Interruptions

Before you start, tell the whole group that anyone who is watching an improvisation can interrupt, join in and leave, at any time they like. Then, with the group divided into pairs, each pair improvises while the rest of the group watches. Use the Complex Scenario Cards and the Character Cards to set up the scene in the normal way, and let an improvisation start. After a minute or two, when the scene is properly established, the rest can join in. The rule is that there should be no more than four people in the scene at any one time, so if a fifth person arrives, one of the others has to leave. Even one of the original pair can leave, but of course, if the improvisation goes on long enough, they, or anyone else, can come back later. The original two improvisers should always come back as the same character they were when they left.

The original two improvisers can also bring other people into the scene by, for instance, calling for the waiter, or knocking on an imaginary door, or (wait for it . . .) making a telephone call. Now that everyone is tuned in to these techniques, the other improvisers who are watching can immediately leap up and be the waiter, or the person answering the door, or *the person on the other end of the telephone*!

(The rule about never having one-sided conversations on a telephone still applies, but now that other people become part of the improvisation, there never needs to be a one-sided conversation.)

RATIONALE   *This kind of group work makes it possible for exploratory improvisations to be taken in all manner of directions, and, although the improvisations can become quite wild, if everyone is able to keep them truthful, then they can also become exciting and unpredictable.*

DEBRIEFING   *Again: Did it stay truthful? If not, where and why did it go wrong? Did people feel free to interrupt at any time, or were they afraid of 'spoiling' the scene? Did the improvisers learn anything about their characters and relationships?*

Introduction to the Extreme Scenario Cards

First of all, explain that some of these Extreme Scenarios may seem to be silly but they are all the basic building blocks of film, TV or theatrical drama. As I said in the Introduction, when the baby alien bursts out of John Hurt's stomach in the film *Alien*, it's not a joke, the actors play the scene with total truth and conviction, resulting in a horrific moment. E.T. makes the audiences cry because he is lost, ill and far from home. Frodo Baggins's quest to throw a ring into a volcano is massively important and scary. So, bearing all that in mind, the improvisers should approach these scenarios with the desire to create the same in-depth emotional reality as the makers of all those films did.

So it's time to crack open the Extreme Scenario Cards and to let the improvisers have fun. They can imagine what it's really like to be aliens from another planet, or goblins in an enchanted forest. They can explore meeting an identical twin for the first time or having a conversation with someone who is invisible. They can discover how they might feel if a nuclear war had just started or if they were a passenger on a sinking ship. They can imagine what it's like to see a ghost and what it might be like to be a ghost!

⚡ Extreme Improvisations with Interruptions

Using the Extreme Improvisation Cards and the Character Cards ask a pair of people to come forward to choose an improvisation. Once they have discovered what they are supposed to improvise and who they are supposed to be, ask the group if anyone else wants to become part of the improvisation. When you start experimenting with these Extreme Scenarios, it's probably better if there are only two or three extra people joining in.

Then, as the group becomes adept at exchanging and swapping focus, more and more of them can become part of the scenario. They can be other passengers on the sinking ship or they can be people in the street or other family members or anything they like. And they can interrupt and create unexpected changes. They can interrupt in pairs. They can take over the improvisation by becoming very high-status characters and arresting everybody (or trying to). They can be foreigners speaking in gobbledegook so that the other improvisers have no idea what they want. They can be silent observers within the scene. They can walk on and walk off like passing strangers who are getting on with their own lives and not become involved in the scene at all.

Once these improvisations have started, anyone can join in and become part of the scene by arriving as a suitable interruption, but here's a couple of rules:

1. IT'S VITAL TO KEEP THESE IMPROVISATIONS TRUTHFUL.

2. EVERYONE IN THE GROUP HAS EQUAL IMPORTANCE ONCE AN IMPROVISATION HAS STARTED.

DEBRIEFING   *Always discuss whether the interruptions were suitable and whether they were integrated correctly into the improvisation. Discuss whether too many people became part of the improvisation and whether it became confusing or not. Also keep a firm hand on the focus of the improvisation. As they get used to these techniques they will be able to develop 'sub-scenes' in the background of an improvisation and they may be able to allow these sub-scenes to become the main focus for a while, but it's important to prevent everyone in the group trying to make their sub-scene the main focus of the improvisation at the same time as every-one else.*

Session Debriefing

The purpose of this session is for the improvisers to learn how to be creative and to discover how far they can 'push' an improvisation without losing the truth and reality of character or situation.

They can have fun. Explore. Find out how other people think. Investigate situations that are unknown to them. Enjoy the creativity of others. Trust their own talent. And get involved.

From now on they should be able to approach any improvisation request without fear. They should respond positively if a director wants to guide an improvised scene in a new direction by asking another improviser to interrupt and join in. They should be able to use improvisation to explore mystery, romance, drama, adventure or any other genre. They should be able to improvise with courage, imagination and creativity. But whatever explorations they make, they will always have a total commitment to the truth and reality of a scene.

IF ACTORS ARE PEOPLE WHO LIKE TO GIVE LIFE AND SUB-
stance to a story, then improvisers are people who like to give
life and substance to their imaginations. They are trying to
harness and control an unbelievably active part of their brains in
order to discover how people behave through *experience* rather
than through the *intellect*. These improvisation sessions make
continual use of the imagination, so it is important that each
session should start with some warm-up games and exercises to
clear the mind from the clutter of day-to-day distractions and
focus the concentration on the job in hand.

In creating a session it is good to do preparatory work that
relates directly to the objectives of the session, so in each chapter I have included appropriate exercises. However, there are a
number of other games and exercises that could be used at the
start of any session because they have no specific outcomes other
than encouraging a suitably creative environment, sharpening
the concentration, getting the blood pumping through the veins,
bonding the group, and preparing everybody for work.

Stanislavsky talks about four major building blocks for creativity
– Naivety, Relaxation, Concentration and Imagination – and I
have grouped the games and exercises in this chapter under
those headings to encourage and stimulate these parts of the
creative process. However, some of the games fulfil the objectives of two or more of these building blocks and could be put
under more than one heading.

I have also included some Improvisation Exercises, which are like practising scales on the piano and can be used regularly to release their imaginations and invigorate their instincts.

Naivety

Clapping Around the Circle

Ask the group to stand in a circle. The first person turns to the person on their right, claps their hands and returns to a neutral position. The next person does the same, and so on round the circle. When it is someone's turn to clap they can clap to the person on their right, on their left, or to someone across the circle, but they must always return to a neutral position. The clapping should always be alert and dynamic.

RATIONALE   *This exercise promotes group awareness, concentration and alertness.*

Zip, Zap, Boing

This is like 'Clapping Around the Circle' except that it is done with the words 'zip', 'zap' and 'boing'. Ask the group to stand in a circle with each person putting their hands palm to palm at chest level. The first person sweeps their hands to the right saying 'zip', and then returns to a neutral position. The next person does the same, and so on round the circle. When it's someone's turn, they can 'zip' to the people on either side of them. If they want to send it to someone across the circle, they have to say 'zap', and use their hands to indicate clearly who they want to send it to. If someone receives a 'zap' from across the circle, they can 'zip' it to either of the people standing next to them, or 'zap' it to someone else across the circle. However, if they send it back to the person who sent it to them they have to make a physical movement as if they are bouncing something off their chest and say 'boing'. Note: You can't 'boing' a 'zip' but you can 'boing' a 'boing'!

RATIONALE   *This exercise promotes group awareness, concentration and alertness. It is also fun to do and helps warm up the group's voices.*

▶ Pass a Movement Around the Circle

This is like 'Clapping Around the Circle' except that the first person does an unusual movement with an accompanying sound, and the next person has to copy both movement and sound and pass it on. At any point someone can send a new movement and sound back round the circle in the other direction. (It's best not to try to send the movement and sound across the circle because it is difficult to be accurate as to who it is being sent to.)

RATIONALE   *This exercise promotes group awareness, concentration and alertness. It is also fun to do and helps warm up the group's voices. It encourages spontaneity and helps them to release their inhibitions.*

▶ Back to Back

With the whole group divided into pairs and all the pairs working at the same time, ask each pair to stand back to back and to get to know each other's backs by moving them around against each other. Then ask them to move around the room with their backs still touching but without talking. They are not allowed to hold on with their arms. Ask them to explore how fast they can move; who leads; the exchange of leadership; whether they can sit on the floor together back to back; whether they can stand up together back to back; what else they can do. The important thing is that they don't talk and they don't use their hands or arms to link together or to help with any of the movements. All the communication is made through the feel of each other's backs.

RATIONALE   *This exercise promotes trust, complicity and physical awareness. It also sharpens their ability to negotiate and communicate.*

▶ Grandmother's Footsteps

This is a traditional children's game which can be adapted for actors.

One person (Grandma) stands at one end of the room facing the wall and the rest of the group go to the other end of the room. On the signal to start, the people in the group have to move forward; however, Grandma can turn round at any time 'she' likes, at which point everyone has to freeze (stand perfectly still). If anyone is seen to be moving, Grandma sends them back to the end of the room to start again. The game ends when one person in the group manages to tap Grandma on the shoulder without being seen. That person is the winner and it then becomes their turn to be Grandma.

Variations:

The group moves down the room with physical expressions of:

1. Murderous intent, freezing in frightening positions

2. Love and adoration, freezing in romantic, loving positions

3. Indifference, freezing as if they don't even know Grandma is there

4. Clowns, freezing in funny positions

5. Giants, freezing as if they were enormous

RATIONALE   *This exercise promotes a sense of fun, physical control, awareness and concentration.*

🂱 Blind Dracula

For this game everyone, including Dracula, has their eyes shut for the whole time. No cheating.

Ask the group to stand in a circle shoulder to shoulder with their eyes shut. Then walk around the outside of the circle and tap one person on their shoulders. This person becomes Dracula but no one else knows who it is. Having done this, ask the whole group, including Dracula, to disperse round the room still without opening their eyes. And then everyone, including Dracula, should feel their way carefully around the room with their hands out in front of them. When Dracula touches another person, he has to put his hands firmly on their shoulders, either from the front or from behind. At which point that person has to let out a blood-curdling scream and then they become a Dracula too. So now there are two Draculas feeling their way around. As the game continues there will be more and more Draculas. If two Draculas put their hands on each other's shoulders at the same time they both have to laugh in a mad, maniacal manner. The game finishes when everyone is a Dracula.

RATIONALE *This exercise promotes a sense of fun, trust and sensory awareness. Also relaxation.*

Relaxation

Down, Down, Baby

Ask everyone to stand in a circle and hold their left hand out to the side, palm down and their right hand to the other side, palm up. By moving their hands up and down everyone can then clap on the hands of the people either side. Ask them to do it at a steady rhythm and then slowly teach them the following sequence of words and actions. If you use four handclaps per line to start with, you will be going at the right speed. The actions are on the capitalised words and when there are no actions they should continue to clap the rhythm on each other's hands.

'Down, Down, Baby,

Down, Down the ROLLER COASTER.*'* (Make a 'roller coaster' movement with your hands from up right to down left, palms together.)

'Sweet, Sweet, Baby,

I'll never LET *you* GO.*'* (Right hand to left shoulder on 'let', left hand to right shoulder on 'go'. Like a hug.)

'Gimme, gimme Coco Pop,

Gimme, gimme ROCK.*'* (Turn to the left, bend knees and thrust hips forward and elbows back.)

'Gimme, gimme Coco Pop,

Gimme, gimme ROCK.*'* (Turn to the right, bend knees and thrust hips forward and elbows back)

'Grandma, Grandma,

Sick in bed,

She sent for the doctor,

The DOCTOR SAID . . . *'* (Shake index finger to the middle of the circle like telling someone off.)

'Let's get the rhythm in the head,

DING DONG.' (Tilt head to the right on 'ding', and to the left on 'dong'.)

'Let's get the rhythm in the head,

DING DONG.' (As above, tilt head from right to left.)

'Let's get the rhythm in the hands.'

(Clap, Clap.)

'Let's get the rhythm in the hands.'

(Clap, Clap.)

'Let's get the rhythm in the feet.'

(Stamp, Stamp.)

'Let's get the rhythm in the feet.'

(Stamp, Stamp.)

'Let's get the rhythm in the HO . . . O – OT DOG.' (Bend knees and rotate hips.)

'Let's get the rhythm in the HO . . . O – OT DOG.' (Bend knees and rotate hips.)

'Put it all together and what have you got?

DING DONG.' (Tilt head from right to left.)

(Clap, Clap.)

(Stamp, Stamp.)

'HO . . . O – OT DOG.' (Bend knees and rotate hips.)

'Put it all backwards and what have you got?

HO . . . O – OT DOG.' (Bend knees and rotate hips.)

(Stamp, Stamp.)

(Clap, Clap.)

'DONG DING.' (Tilt head from left to right.)

(Note: the 'Ding Dong' is reversed in the last line and so is the tilting of the head.)

RATIONALE *Although this is complicated to explain, it is great fun to do. Once a group has learned it, it is a quick way to warm them up. It sharpens their attention, gets them physically moving and bonds the group.*

Persecutor/Protector

Ask everyone to walk around the room, in and out of each other, heading towards the emptier parts of the room as much as they can. While they are doing this, ask each person to think of someone in the room and, without letting it be obvious, try to keep as far away from that person as they can. Once everyone is moving around trying to avoid their 'persecutors', ask them to think of someone else (preferably someone up the other end of the room), and try to get as close to this second person as they can, while, at the same time, they are still trying to avoid the first person. They can move as quickly as they like, but they must never make it obvious to either person that they have chosen them.

RATIONALE *This game creates a strange and unexpected flow of movement around the room. They have to concentrate on two different people at the same time and respond accordingly. They have to deal with the problem of their persecutor and their protector both standing next to each other. Sometimes they find themselves trying to avoid the person that wants to get close to them; sometimes they are trying to get close to a person that keeps running away. It's very exciting as they are forced to run, stop, walk, watch and respond.*

Zombies

Ask everyone to walk around the room, in and out of each other, and be zombies (the living dead). They must develop a slow but relentless zombie walk and a death-like zombie sound – a howl or a groan. Then ask them all to be versions of Frankenstein's monster in the same way. Then 'The Mummy'. But each time they have to create a different slow, but relentless walk and a death-like sound.

RATIONALE *This is an exercise in control and creativity, but I really use it as a preparation for 'Chair Rush' (see below), because I want them to get used to the concept of a slow and relentless way of walking.*

▓ Chair Rush

First of all, practise 'Zombies' with everyone.

Then ask each person to place one chair somewhere in the room so that all the chairs are haphazardly scattered about. When they have done that, each person should sit on their chair. Then ask one person to leave their chair and go to the far end of the room. That person then has to walk towards the empty chair like a zombie and try to sit on it. They can't run; they have to do a slow relentless zombie walk and make a death-like sound. Everyone else has to prevent the zombie sitting on the empty chair. One of them can do this by getting up, moving as fast as they like, towards the empty chair and sitting on it. However, once they move they will leave behind another empty chair that the zombie can now walk towards and try to sit on, so someone else has to move onto that chair, leaving behind their empty chair which the zombie can now walk towards . . . etc. Several people will often leave their chairs at the same time. When this happens the zombie can head towards any of the empty chairs. Once someone has left their chair, they can't go back to it. When the zombie eventually manages to sit on an empty chair, the game is over, and someone else becomes the zombie. I usually choose the person who seems to be responsible for letting the zombie win.

RATIONALE *As they play this game, they realise that they have to work as a team otherwise it is too easy for the zombie. Once the teamwork is happening, the game creates a flow of movement around the room that becomes very difficult for the zombie to handle until someone makes a mistake.*

▓ Anyone Who . . .

Ask everyone to get a chair and sit in a circle except one person who stands in the middle of the circle. There are no spare chairs. The person in the middle then says something true about themselves, starting with the phrase 'Anyone who . . . ', such as: 'Anyone who had tea for breakfast this morning,' or 'Anyone who likes The Beatles,' or 'Anyone who is wearing trainers.' If that is true for anyone else in the circle then they have to get up and move to another chair. The person in the middle has to try to get in an empty chair while everyone is moving around. Whoever can't find an empty chair now stands in the middle and we start again.

Rules:

1. Whatever the person in the middle says has to be true about them.

2. If it's true of anyone in the circle, they have to move to a different chair.

3. Once someone stands up, they can't go back to the chair they were in before.

RATIONALE   *This game is very bonding for the group as they realise that they have similar likes and dislikes. It's also fun to think up embarrassing things like: 'Anyone who was a Spice Girls fan when they were thirteen.' Or 'Anyone who likes to sort out jelly beans according to their colour.'*

Wink Murder

Ask everyone to stand in a circle shoulder to shoulder with their eyes shut. Then walk around the circle and tap one person on their shoulder. That person then becomes the murderer without anyone else knowing who it is. Having done that, ask everyone to open their eyes and walk around the room weaving in and out of each other. The murderer 'kills' people by surreptitiously winking at them. When a person is winked at, they have to count slowly and silently to five as they continue to walk and then they have to perform a 'death'. It's important that they *count slowly* to five before dying so the murderer can move away from the scene of the crime. After someone has 'died' they have to go to the side of the room and watch. The object of the game is for everyone to guess the murderer before they are all 'killed'. Anyone can accuse anyone at any time but the game only stops when *everyone* who is left agrees who they think the murderer is. (Except the accused of course.) However, the murderer should never give themselves up until *everyone* is accusing him or her. The murderer can lie and cheat and accuse other people of being the murderer, and, in fact, do *anything* to put people off the scent.

Once everyone has decided to accuse one person, then the murderer has to own up. If the murderer is the person they have all accused, then the group have won. If the murderer is someone else, then the murderer has won.

RATIONALE   *This game is very bonding for the group and it stimulates their observation skills. It is also great fun for them to do and is one of the most popular warm-up games.*

🔥 Stuck in the Mud

This is like 'Tag'. One person chases the rest of the group round the room. When they touch someone, that person has to stand with their legs apart and their arms stretched upwards like an X, shout 'Stuck in the mud,' and stay in that position. Anyone from the rest of the group can release a person who is 'stuck in the mud' by crawling between their legs. It's quite good to get two people to chase, or to keep changing the chaser because it is a very exhausting game!

RATIONALE   *This game is a great physical warm-up for the group and it promotes a strong sense of co-operation.*

🔥 Concentration

🔥 1, 2, 3

Two people face each other. The first person says 'one', the second: 'two', the first: 'three', the second says 'one', the first: 'two', etc. They keep counting to three taking it in turns to say the numbers. Once they've done that, they think up a gesture and a sound that they can both use to replace the word 'two'. For instance, they could replace it with a jump and a 'ha!' so it would now go 'one', jump-'ha!', 'three', 'one', jump-'ha!', 'three', etc. When they have mastered that, ask them to keep their replacement for the word 'two', and find a completely different replacement for the word 'three'. Again, let them practise. Then ask them to find a third sound and gesture to replace the word 'one', so there are no numbers being said at all; just sounds and gestures.

RATIONALE   *This exercise sharpens their concentration and ability to work together. It also helps them learn how to negotiate their creative ideas.*

How Far Can We Count?

Everyone stands in a circle. With one person at a time saying a number, the group counts from 'one' to as high as they can. Anyone in the circle can say whichever number comes next, but if two or more people say it at the same time, they have to stop and start at 'one' again.

RATIONALE   *This exercise promotes group awareness, concentration and sensitivity to their surroundings.*

Noises in a Circle

Everyone stands in a circle with their eyes shut and makes a repeatable noise. While making their own noise, each person should listen to the two noises on either side of them and try to get to know them. Still keeping their eyes shut, ask everyone to spread out into the room carefully, and start making their noises again. The object is to try to re-form the circle just by listening to the sounds that everyone is making.

RATIONALE   *This exercise promotes trust and sensory awareness. It is also fun to do, and gives them a great sense of delight when the circle is successfully reformed.*

Ballerina/Bouncer

The group stands in a circle with one person in the middle. The person in the middle has to point at someone and say 'Ballerina' or 'Bouncer', or any of the other words in the list below. (They all begin with the letter B.) At that point the person being pointed to, together with the two people on either side, have to mime the action specified and make the appropriate noises:

Word	'Ballerina'
Pointed-at person	Does a pirouette and sings 'The Sugar Plum Fairy'.

People either side	Stretch one leg back and the opposite arm forward.
Word	'Bouncer'
Pointed-at person	Steps forward, folds arms and says, 'What choo want?'
People either side	Step forward behind the centre person and say, 'Yeah!'
Word	'Boxer'
Pointed-at person	Falls to the floor as if knocked out.
People either side	Count like referees, saying, 'A-one, A-two, A-three.'
Word	'Bond'
Pointed-at person	Puts gun to cheek. Says 'The name's Bond. James Bond.'
People either side	Drape themselves on Bond like sexy 'Bond girls'. Squeal.
Word	'Bat'
Pointed-at person	Uses first fingers to make teeth. Makes high-pitched 'eeks'.
People either side	Flap their arms and say 'Frrr . . . Frrr . . . Frrr'.
Word	'Banana'
Pointed-at person	Puts arms above their head. Bends body into banana shape.
People either side	Unpeels the 'banana' like monkeys. Making monkey noises.
Word	'Biggles'
Pointed-at person	Makes goggles with fingers. Hums 'Dam Busters March'.
Person to left	Uses arms like wings of a plane and makes flying movement.
Person to right	Uses arms to create Biggles' scarf blowing in the wind.

Word	'Baby'
Pointed-at person	Rocks baby in arms. Sings 'Rock-a-Bye Baby'.
People either side	Rub knuckles into their eyes. Cry like babies.
Word	'Bimbo'
Pointed-at person	Stands like Marilyn Monroe holding skirt from blowing up.
People either side	Giggle, bend knees and shake shoulders.
Word	'Bicycle'
Pointed-at person	Puts hands on handlebars, says, 'Ding Ding'.
Person to left	Moves feet as though pedalling.
Person to right	Makes a wheel shape with arm.

As soon as anyone makes a mistake, or hesitates for too long, they have to go into the centre.

RATIONALE   *This exercise promotes alertness and spontaneity. It is also a splendid physical and vocal warm-up, great fun to do and is very popular.*

Imagination

Coil of Rope

Everyone stands in a circle with their arms around each other's shoulders. Then they have to imagine that they are standing at the top of a tower made from an enormous coil of rope. The coil of rope is rather unsteady, so they have to keep their balance, and be extremely careful as they move. They then have two minutes to rearrange themselves in the order of the first letter of their first names without falling off the tower of rope.

RATIONALE   *This exercise stimulates their imaginations. It is also excellent for encouraging physical contact and complicity.*

In the Manner of the Word

This is a traditional parlour game and is played in Act Two of Noël Coward's play, *Hay Fever*.

Everyone sits in a circle. One person leaves the room and the rest decide on an adverb. (Usually a word with ' . . . ly' at the end as in 'quickly' or 'passionately' or 'mysteriously'.) Once the group have decided on a word, the other person comes back into the room and stands in the middle of the circle. He or she then has to ask people to perform actions 'in the manner of the word,' as in: 'Dance in the manner of the word.' 'Make a cup of tea in the manner of the word.' 'Recite a poem in the manner of the word.' 'Ask the person next to you to lend you some money in the manner of the word.' The person in the middle can either give the instructions one at a time around the circle, or ask anyone in any order. It depends how integrated the group is. The questioner is allowed three guesses and can make their guesses at any time.

RATIONALE   *This exercise promotes observation, creativity and mental stimulation.*

Ball Games Without a Ball

Creating an Imaginary Ball

With everyone working at the same time but each person working on their own, ask everyone to imagine they have a tennis ball. They should bounce it and see how high it bounces; throw it at the wall and try to catch it; feel how soft the surface is; feel how spongy it is; feel its weight. They need to get to know everything about the ball until they can confidently imagine they have it in their hands. Then ask them to do the same sort of things with a football. Then the same sort of things with a table-tennis ball. A squash ball. A beach ball. A foam rubber ball. And so on. Then ask each person to choose any kind of ball they like and start exploring it and using it like before. Ultimately, they need to find the best way to play with their imaginary ball, whether it's to bounce it or kick it or throw it in the air or whatever.

Swapping Imaginary Balls

(This is a continuation of 'Creating an Imaginary Ball'.) When everyone has discovered the best way to play with their imaginary ball, they should now stick with that, whether it's a bounce or a kick or a toss in the air. They should then find someone to pair up with. Still playing with their imaginary balls, each person should watch the other and get to know how they play with theirs. When they are ready, they should mime swapping the imaginary balls and then go off playing with their new ball. Then they should find someone else to pair up with, examine what the new person is doing, and mime swapping again. This can continue until everyone has swapped about four or five times. Now they have to try to find their original ball by negotiating and swapping with the others in the room. (I have played this game lots of times and there are always two or three people who never get their ball back!)

Imaginary Volleyball

Another ball game without a ball is simply having four people play beach volleyball, or handball. It's worth mentioning to them that acting having *lost* a point is just as interesting as acting having *won* a point, since it isn't a real game, and there is no actual ball. There is a danger that they all want to win, so they mime returning every single shot and the point goes on for ever!

RATIONALE *These exercises stimulate imaginations, sharpen their observation and negotiation skills, and help refine their visual memory.*

Improvisation Exercises

Story Around the Circle, a Word at a Time

Ask the group to stand in a circle and make up a story which progresses round the circle with each person adding one word when it comes to their turn.

After they have practised for a bit, they should be encouraged to say the first word that comes into their heads, rather than trying to think up clever and witty words.

RATIONALE   *This exercise is to stop people censoring their own imaginations. They have to try to stop being in control and allow their instinct to take over. They have to learn to 'feel the force'.*

Story Around and Across the Circle

This is the same as 'Story Around the Circle, a Word at a Time', except it works like 'Zip, Zap, Boing'.

Standing in a neutral position with the hands palm to palm at the level of their chests, the first person sweeps their hands towards the person on the right saying the first word of the story. Then, when it's their turn, each person can 'send' their word in either direction or across the circle indicating who they want to go next by the direction in which they point their hands. And so on.

RATIONALE   *As above, this exercise is teaching them to be instinctive, but it also sharpens their concentration because they have no idea when they will be the next person to add a word.*

Story Anywhere at Any Time

Ask the group to stand in a circle with one person in the middle. As above, the story progresses one word at a time, but for this exercise, the person in the middle points to anyone in the circle at any time for the next word. They can even point to the same person two times in a row.

RATIONALE   *Again, this exercise is really just a variation of the above exercises. It teaches them to be instinctive, it sharpens their concentration and they have absolutely no idea whether they will be the next person required to add a word.*

⚡ Story Around the Circle, a Phrase at a Time

Ask the group to stand in a circle and make up a story which progresses round the circle with each person adding a phrase when it comes to their turn. The phrase doesn't have to be a whole sentence, but it should be a completed thought. It is best if the story is told in the third person, as in:

'A little boy called David was walking down the road . . . '

'He saw a ginger cat . . . '

'The ginger cat was called Tom . . . '

'David hated cats . . . '

'But he liked Tom . . . '

RATIONALE   *This is a progression from the previous two exercises, and it encourages them to use their instincts to add whole ideas to a story, rather than contributing to a given idea with just a single word.*

'Story Around and Across the Circle' and 'Story Anywhere at Any Time' can both be played using a whole phrase instead of a single word.

⚡ Fortunately/Unfortunately

This is similar to the 'Story Around the Circle, a Phrase at a Time' but in this case they should start their phrase with, alternately, the word 'Fortunately' or 'Unfortunately,' as in:

'A little boy called David was walking down the road . . . '

'Fortunately it was a sunny day . . . '

'Unfortunately *he tripped over a piece of wood and grazed his knee . . .* '

'Fortunately *he had a handkerchief to tie round the injury . . .* '

'Unfortunately *the handkerchief was dirty . . .* '

RATIONALE   *This exercise is a variation on the previous exercises and is purely to add variety to a session, so they feel they are doing something a bit different.*

⚡ Two People Talking at the Same Time

Divide the group into pairs and ask all the pairs to work at the same time. This is rather like 'Mirrors' (see Chapter 13: Releasing the Imagination) except it is done with words rather than actions. Two people face each other, and as one person speaks slowly, the other has to try to say exactly the same words at the same time. Then they reverse roles. After they have practised that, explain that from now on, neither of them is the leader. They must do the same exercise and continually swap the lead. When one person starts to say a phrase, the other can take over and continue it quite differently, and even before it's finished, the first person can take control again and lead it in a new direction. All the time they are both trying to speak simultaneously. When that is working, ask each pair – talking as one person – to try to have a conversation with another pair, who will also be talking as one person.

RATIONALE   *This is an exercise in complicity and concentration, but since it uses words rather than movement, it helps them to work together in the creation of ideas.*

⚡ Gobbledegook

Gobbledegook is simply the use of meaningless made-up words that sound like a foreign language. It's quite hard for some people to do. The easiest way into this is for them to practise repeating explosive consonants with changing vowel sounds as in: 'Pa, pa, pa, pa. Po, po, po, po. Boo, boo, boo, boo.' They can use 't', 'k', 'rrr', 'v', 'm', even 'sh', 'l', or 'w'. Anything, as long as they follow it with changing vowel sounds. Then they can start stringing them together like 'Pi . . . li . . .

ko . . . sham . . . si . . . tuk. Fi . . . ka . . . pa . . . too. So . . . ti . . . mi . . . no . . . sa . . . tub.' And pretty soon they are talking gobbledegook. It's fun for two people to have a conversation speaking in gobbledegook because they immediately sound like a couple of very passionate Eastern Europeans.

RATIONALE   *Using gobbledegook instead of a real language means they have to use their voices and their physicality in a more expressive manner in order to communicate their ideas and thoughts.*

So there we have a handful of useful games and exercises. There are, of course, countless books of games and exercises that are helpful in structuring classes and I have to acknowledge that very few of the games in this last chapter are my own invention. I have plundered the ideas of Anna Scher, Augusto Boal, Clive Barker, Keith Johnstone and many others, and I expect other people will plunder my ideas in the same way. There is a pool of acting warm-ups that have become part of the arsenal of games and exercises used by drama teachers and workshop leaders all over the world, and it is good to tap into that common knowledge and even add to it.

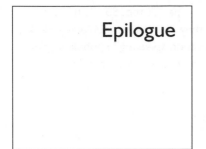

Epilogue

TO ALL TEACHERS AND WORKSHOP LEADERS LOOKING FOR a manual of exercises and ideas, I hope this book and these cards are useful and the exercises are clearly explained. For directors, I hope you are encouraged to harness the power of improvisation as a rehearsal tool. And as for the people who might have used this book to explore their own imaginations and talents, all I have to say is:

Go forth and improvise.

*Unleash your imagination from
the chains of inhibition.*

Trust your own talent and individuality.

And above all – KEEP IT REAL!

The Improvisation Cards

Preparing the Cards

The ninety-six Improvisation Cards in this book have been printed at a distance from the spine so that they can be cut out with ease, and without the book falling apart. It'll be a bit thinner, but it will still be a book.

1.   Probably the best way to create useable cards is to cut them out along the dotted lines and laminate them. If you don't have a laminator, most high-street printing shops should offer the service. Laminating the cards makes the process slightly more time-consuming, but will give the cards longevity. I suggest that the lamination overlaps the edge of the card and the corners are snipped off, making the cards easier to handle and more resilient.

2.   If there is no laminator available, the cards can just be cut out and used as they are. They may be slightly flimsier, but with careful handling, they can easily be shuffled and used on a regular basis. If you do this, I suggest that you snip the corners as suggested above.

3.   Finally, for those people who don't like the idea of chopping up books, the card pages can be photocopied. I would suggest that they are printed on different coloured card for each category so they are easily distinguishable. With careful positioning, you will be able to photocopy the information on one side and the backing on the other.

Characters

- Addict
- Ambitious person
- Bossy person
- Competitive person
- Compulsive liar
- Contrary person
- Person at a Crossroads
- Do-gooder
- Egoist
- Elusive person
- Expert
- Fallen star
- Generous person
- Guilt-ridden person
- Holidaymaker
- Hypochondriac
- Indecisive person

- Lazy person
- Leader
- Loner
- Lover
- Melancholic
- Optimist
- Perfectionist
- Physical person
- Romantic
- Searcher
- Servile person
- Shy person
- Sycophant
- Vain person
- Victim
- Winner

S Simple Scenarios

- A job interview
- A customer and a shop assistant
- A blind date
- A teacher and a student
- Strangers in an all-night café at 5.00 in the morning
- Flat-sharers on their first evening in a new flat
- A hairdresser and a client
- Live-in partners at breakfast
- Strangers sitting next to each other on a bus
- Homeless people
- People having a break at work
- People on a platform waiting for a train

- People in a hospital waiting room
- Painters and decorators
- People in a gym
- An employer and a new employee on their first day at work
- People at an airport, waiting to get on a delayed flight
- Friends meeting for an evening out. One person is an hour late
- Siblings meeting for a drink
- People by a swimming pool in Spain
- Friends camping in the woods

Complex Scenarios

- Strangers trapped in a cellar after an earthquake

- A parent and a grown-up child meet after fifteen years apart

- An armed householder discovers a burglar

- People lost in the woods settle down for the night

- A householder and a plumber, electrician or repair person, etc.

- People in a jail cell. One has been there for ten years, the other arrived today

- A kidnapper and a victim

- The partner and the lover of a dead person meet after the funeral

- A television host and a celebrity meeting just before a television interview

- A boss giving a trusted employee the sack for economic reasons

- A fan has won dinner with a famous person

- Two parents of different children meet at a school parents' evening

- A customer and a barman/barwoman in a quiet pub

- Musicians in a successful band disagree about the future

- Extras on a film set

- A step-parent and an adult stepchild with nothing in common

- Ex-partners meeting after five years

- Two ex-partners of the same person meet in the street

- A long-term couple, breaking up, divide their belongings

- Strangers stuck in a lift

- A musician and his/her manager after a gig

IE Extreme Scenarios

- A person tries to rob a bank
- Father Christmas (or Mother Christmas) and an elf on Christmas Eve
- Identical twins meet for the first time
- A wounded soldier is cared for by a friendly enemy civilian
- Aliens from a different planet arrive on Earth (looking like humans)
- Passengers on a ship which slowly starts to sink
- A person who has become invisible tries to talk to a friend about it
- People watching the news on TV which says a nuclear war has started
- People who have just been shipwrecked on a desert island
- A meeting between a superhero and an evil villain

- A person and a ghost
- People who seem to be the only survivors after a nuclear holocaust
- Astronauts who have survived massive damage to their spaceship
- A wild-west outlaw and a heroic cowboy (or cowgirl)
- Time travellers go backwards or forwards in time in their time machine
- Iron-age cave-dwellers (who can speak)
- A ship's captain rescues a person who has been shipwrecked for ten years
- Mountaineers on Everest. One is injured
- Goblins in an enchanted forest
- People drink a shrinking potion
- Witches/wizards make spells or create a potion
- Wildcard: make up your own!

Index of Games and Exercises

The Improvisation Cards

▓ Exercises

Improvisations

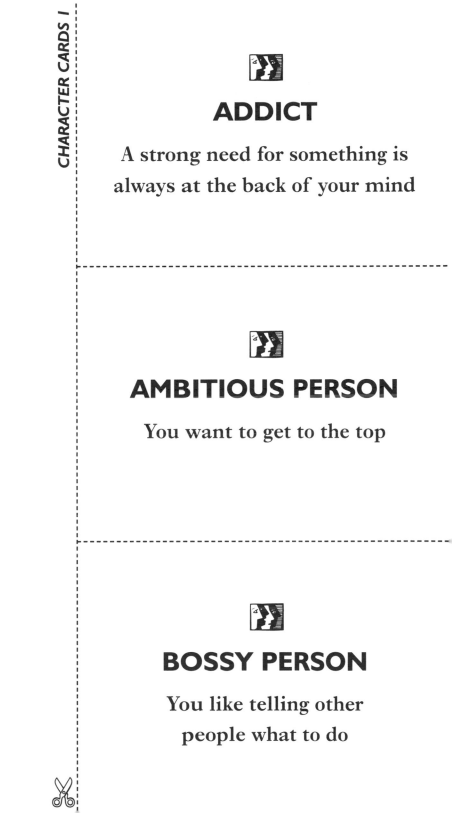

ADDICT

A strong need for something is always at the back of your mind

AMBITIOUS PERSON

You want to get to the top

BOSSY PERSON

You like telling other people what to do

CHARACTER

CHARACTER

CHARACTER

COMPETITIVE PERSON

You want to be the best

COMPULSIVE LIAR

You continually make up lies
about yourself and your past

CONTRARY PERSON

You tend to disagree
with everything

CHARACTER

CHARACTER

CHARACTER

PERSON AT A CROSSROADS

You have to make an important decision about something in your life

---

DO-GOODER

You are always trying to help other peoplc

EGOIST

You have a great deal of confidence in yourself

CHARACTER

CHARACTER

CHARACTER

ELUSIVE PERSON

You don't really like
people trying to pin you
down or categorise you

EXPERT

You feel you can talk intelligently
about most things

FALLEN STAR

You were famous once
but not any more

CHARACTER

CHARACTER

CHARACTER

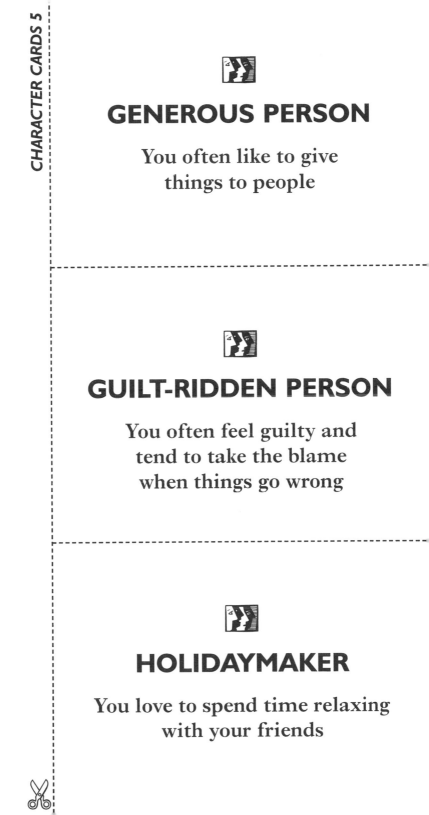

GENEROUS PERSON

You often like to give
things to people

GUILT-RIDDEN PERSON

You often feel guilty and
tend to take the blame
when things go wrong

HOLIDAYMAKER

You love to spend time relaxing
with your friends

CHARACTER

CHARACTER

CHARACTER

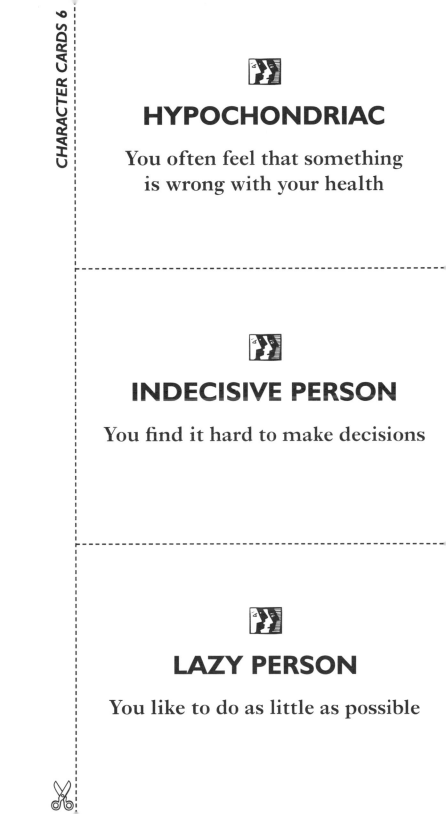

HYPOCHONDRIAC

You often feel that something
is wrong with your health

INDECISIVE PERSON

You find it hard to make decisions

LAZY PERSON

You like to do as little as possible

CHARACTER

CHARACTER

CHARACTER

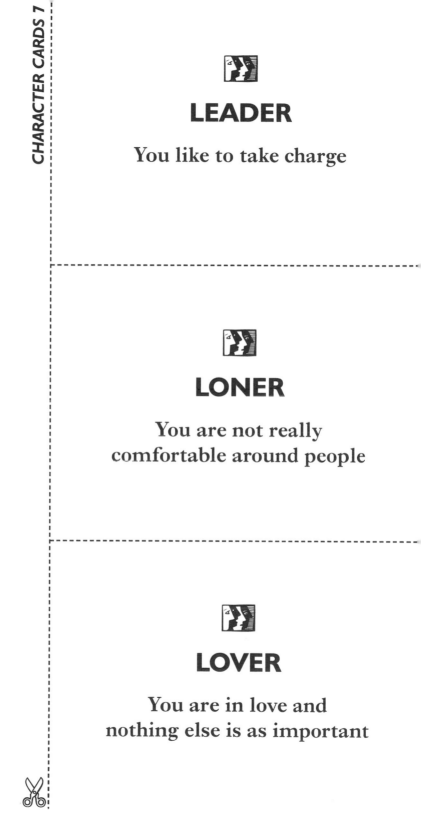

LEADER

You like to take charge

LONER

You are not really
comfortable around people

LOVER

You are in love and
nothing else is as important

CHARACTER

CHARACTER

CHARACTER

MELANCHOLIC

You often get sad about things

OPTIMIST

You always feel things will work out for the best

PERFECTIONIST

You want everything to be perfect

CHARACTER

CHARACTER

CHARACTER

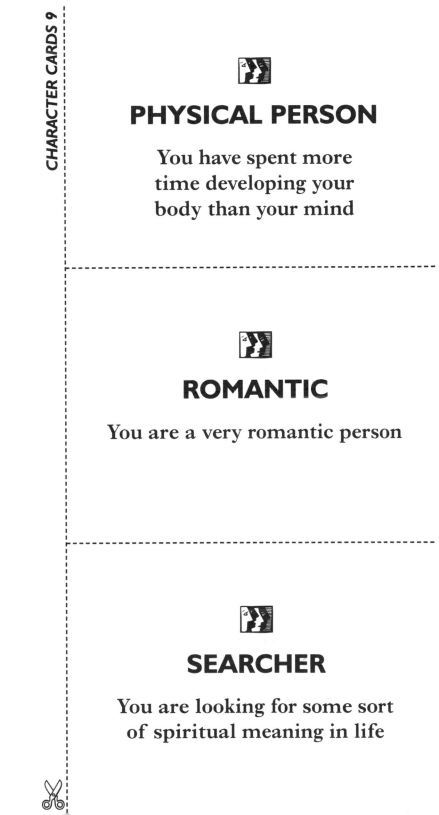

PHYSICAL PERSON

You have spent more
time developing your
body than your mind

ROMANTIC

You are a very romantic person

SEARCHER

You are looking for some sort
of spiritual meaning in life

CHARACTER

CHARACTER

CHARACTER

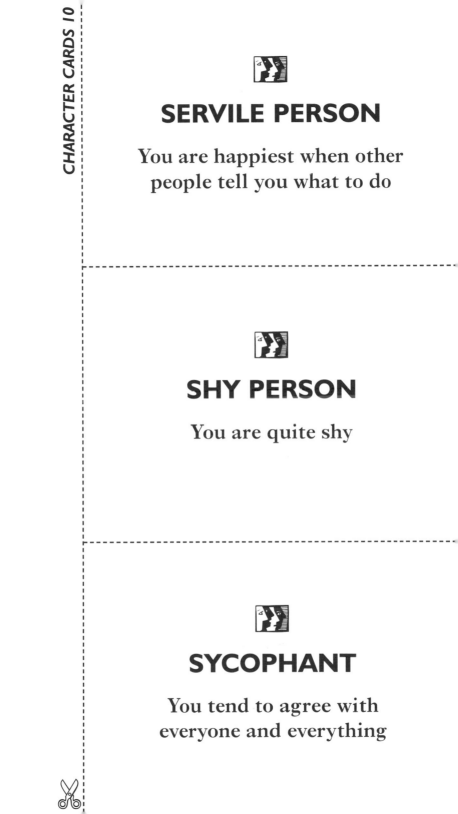

SERVILE PERSON

You are happiest when other people tell you what to do

SHY PERSON

You are quite shy

SYCOPHANT

You tend to agree with everyone and everything

CHARACTER

CHARACTER

CHARACTER

VAIN PERSON

Your appearance is the most
important thing in your life

VICTIM

You feel as if your life
has gone wrong and that
it probably always will

WINNER

You feel as if things
often go right for you

CHARACTER

CHARACTER

CHARACTER

S

A customer and
a shop assistant

S

A teacher
and a student

S

A job interview

S

A blind date

S SIMPLE SCENARIO

S SIMPLE SCENARIO

S SIMPLE SCENARIO

S SIMPLE SCENARIO

S

Flat-sharers on their
first evening in a new flat

S

Live-in partners
at breakfast

S

Strangers in an all-night
café at 5.00 in the morning

S

A hairdresser
and a client

S

SIMPLE SCENARIO

S

SIMPLE SCENARIO

S

SIMPLE SCENARIO

S

SIMPLE SCENARIO

S

Homeless people

S

People on a platform
waiting for a train

S

Strangers sitting next to
each other on a bus

S

People having a break at work

S

SIMPLE SCENARIO

S

SIMPLE SCENARIO

S

SIMPLE SCENARIO

S

SIMPLE SCENARIO

S

Painters and decorators

S

An employer and a new employee on their first day at work

S

People in a hospital waiting room

S

People in a gym

S
SIMPLE SCENARIO

S
SIMPLE SCENARIO

S
SIMPLE SCENARIO

S
SIMPLE SCENARIO

S

Friends meeting for an evening out.
One person is an hour late

S

People by a swimming
pool in Spain

S

People at an airport, waiting
to get on a delayed flight

S

Siblings meeting for a drink

S

SIMPLE SCENARIO

S

SIMPLE SCENARIO

S

SIMPLE SCENARIO

S

SIMPLE SCENARIO

C

A parent and a grown-up child
meet after fifteen years apart

C

An armed householder
discovers a burglar

C

Strangers trapped in a cellar
after an earthquake

S

Friends camping in the woods

COMPLEX SCENARIO

C

COMPLEX SCENARIO

COMPLEX SCENARIO

C

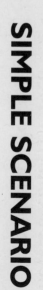

COMPLEX SCENARIO

SIMPLE SCENARIO

S

SIMPLE SCENARIO

C

A householder and a plumber, electrician or repair person, etc.

C

A kidnapper and a victim

C

People lost in the woods settle down for the night

C

People in a jail cell. One has been there for ten years, the other arrived today

COMPLEX SCENARIO

COMPLEX SCENARIO

COMPLEX SCENARIO

COMPLEX SCENARIO

C

A television host and a
celebrity meeting just before
a television interview

C

A fan has won dinner
with a famous person

C

The partner and the lover
of a dead person meet
after the funeral

C

A boss giving a trusted
employee the sack for
economic reasons

COMPLEX SCENARIO

COMPLEX SCENARIO

COMPLEX SCENARIO

COMPLEX SCENARIO

C

A customer and a
barman/barwoman
in a quiet pub

C

Extras on a film set

C

Two parents of different children
meet at a school parents' evening

C

Musicians in a successful band
disagree about the future

COMPLEX SCENARIO

COMPLEX SCENARIO

COMPLEX SCENARIO

COMPLEX SCENARIO

C

Ex-partners meeting
after five years

C

A long-term couple, breaking up,
divide their belongings

C

A step-parent and an adult stepchild
with nothing in common

C

Two ex-partners of the same
person meet in the street

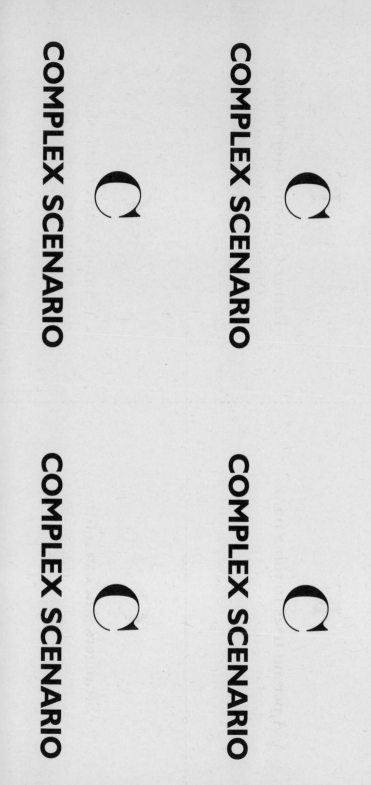

COMPLEX SCENARIO

COMPLEX SCENARIO

COMPLEX SCENARIO

COMPLEX SCENARIO

E

Father Christmas (or Mother Christmas) and an elf on Christmas Eve

C

A musician and his/her manager after a gig

E

A person tries to rob a bank

C

Strangers stuck in a lift

EXTREME SCENARIO

E

C

COMPLEX SCENARIO

EXTREME SCENARIO

E

C

COMPLEX SCENARIO

E

A wounded soldier is cared
for by a friendly enemy civilian

E

Passengers on a ship
which slowly starts to sink

E

Identical twins meet
for the first time

E

Aliens from a different planet
arrive on Earth (looking like humans)

EXTREME SCENARIO

EXTREME SCENARIO

EXTREME SCENARIO

EXTREME SCENARIO

E

People watching the news on TV which says a nuclear war has started

E

A meeting between a superhero and an evil villain

E

A person who has become invisible tries to talk to a friend about it

E

People who have just been shipwrecked on a desert island

EXTREME SCENARIO

 EXTREME SCENARIO

 EXTREME SCENARIO

 EXTREME SCENARIO

IE

People who seem to be the only survivors after a nuclear holocaust

IE

A wild-west outlaw and a heroic cowboy (or cowgirl)

IE

A person and a ghost

IE

Astronauts who have survived massive damage to their spaceship

EXTREME SCENARIO

EXTREME SCENARIO

EXTREME SCENARIO

E

Iron-age cave-dwellers
(who can speak)

E

Mountaineers on Everest.
One is injured

E

Time travellers go backwards
or forwards in time in
their time machine

E

A ship's captain rescues a person who
has been shipwrecked for ten years

EXTREME SCENARIO

EXTREME SCENARIO

EXTREME SCENARIO

EXTREME SCENARIO

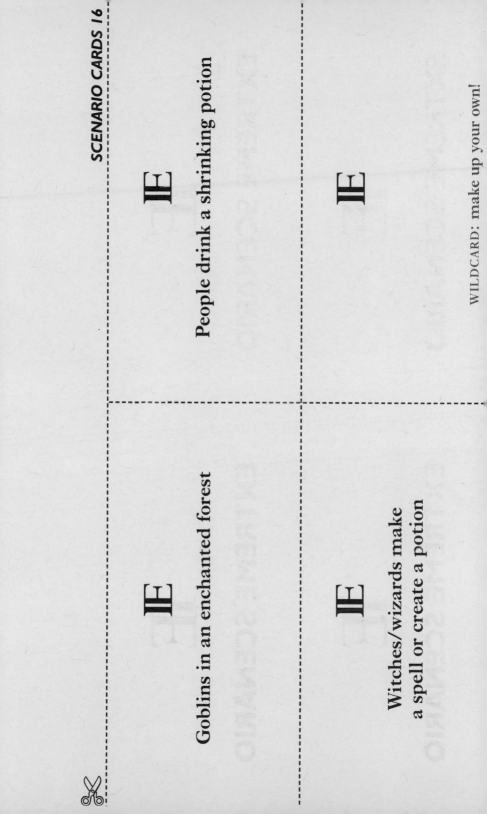

Goblins in an enchanted forest

People drink a shrinking potion

Witches/wizards make
a spell or create a potion

WILDCARD: make up your own!

EXTREME SCENARIO

EXTREME SCENARIO

EXTREME SCENARIO

EXTREME SCENARIO

EXTREME SCENARIO